T0150090

MY FAMILY NEEDS MY

Spiritual Leadership Now

Kristin Panek

**FOUNDER OF
FLOWERING HEART CENTER**

MY FAMILY NEEDS **MY SPIRITUAL LEADERSHIP NOW**
A Guide to Being Your Family's Spiritual Support
Kristin Panek, founder of the Flowering Heart Center

Difference Press, Washington, D.C., USA

ISBN 978-1-68309-270-4

Cover Design: Jennifer Stimson
Editor: Cory Hott

DP
DIFFERENCE
PRESS

ADVANCE PRAISE

"Spiritual teacher Kristin Panek has written an important book about how to be the loving, connected, calm, and happy parent your heart always desired, without having to do anything more. Her loving guidance takes you on a journey of self-discovery so that you can be yourself. Your true and conscious self is the only source of love and connection that is needed for the well-being of your family."

~ Mariana Gigea, MD, Pediatrician ~

"Kudos to Kristin for not only transforming her own life, but also empowering others, through her wisdom, to become spiritual leaders for themselves, their children and their families. It is essential in these times to have the psycho-spiritual tools and skills to successfully navigate life's ups and downs."

~ Dr. Basha Kaplan, PsyD, Clinical Psychologist,
Author, and Public Speaker ~

To my mother, Elizabeth Cunningham, who inspired me through her embodiment of such a deep level of faith.

To my husband, Frank Panek, for his unconditional love and true partnership.

To my children, Kara and Kevin Peters, whom I love so deeply that I was continually inspired to do whatever it took to become a more conscious human being.

To my father, Francis Cunningham, who taught me that I could accomplish whatever I set my mind on.

TABLE OF CONTENTS

FOREWORD

Kristin and I have been friends for nearly a decade. When she asked me to serve on the Board of the Flowering Heart Center, I remember feeling I had to step up to support her, not even sure what I getting myself into. It has been an extraordinary experience and honor, for what has been formed is far beyond what is usually found in our society. This is a community of deep and authentic support, a door that is always open, and when you enter there is no judgment that enters with you. Kristin and her husband Frank lead this community strongly, and truly "walk the walk."

As I read Kristin's words on spiritual leadership, I think of how changed the world would be if all parents, employers, and – quite frankly – any person wishing to be more present would follow the guidance she offers here. There is much wisdom in these pages, and practicing only a few of her suggestions would undoubtedly bring not only a shift in personal perspectives, but a lasting ripple to our world. We all struggle with wanting change, yet as Kristin points out (and lives as an example), change does not just happen in the world. It happens within you. From my experience, it is so easy to blame others for my disappointments and misfortunes, but as Kristin writes, looking inward rather than outward provides answers that you might not have even considered. Seeing yourself and your relationships clearly, and finding a source of power within, as Kristin states and my experience dictates, is the only way to survive in a world that upon first look can seem senseless and meaningless.

I read Kristin's book with excitement for her in my heart. She has finally brought her experience, insights, and personal stories to one place. I have seen her stand in her convictions on what she was called to do in this world, regardless of many contrary opinions. There were times when I was not sure a program would fill up, the center would find a larger space, or Kristin would be able to withstand her schedule, yet those things all have happened. Kristin lives as she teaches and knows what she knows. Going back to the day I said, "yes" to joining Kristin in her endeavor to establish the Center, and looking at what has been created since, have been a powerful reminder to me and many others to 'keep the faith of their intentions' and most of all to believe in miracles. I stood up to support Kristin, but as her book points out, we ultimately serve each other. I became a witness to the power of her intention and faith, for all she had felt was hers to do, is done. Yes, there have been trying moments and times that appeared to move too slowly. Yet, as I think back through the years of our friendship, Kristin's visions have all come to pass.

It seems effortless in hindsight. I know as her friend it did not always feel this way, but regardless, she did not question.

She kept walking in the direction of her inner guidance and has transformed many lives along the way. No doubt this book is Kristin's next step in the journey to open people up to discover what is possible when we live from the inside out.

~ Dawn Sprong ~
Founder of Made As Intended and Village Children's Academy

Chapter 1

A MOMENT OF TRUTH

Laura's Story

Many people find their way to the Flowering Heart Center (FHC) because they struggle with anxiety, depression, or relationship issues. They might feel there is an emptiness inside, as if something is missing. When Laura walked through the door, the similarities between our journeys struck me. I realized there were others who had the experience of realizing they weren't aware of what they truly believed and what they were passing on to their children. Some just rush right past this realization and figure they will deal with it later. Others, like me and Laura, are struck dead in their tracks wondering if they are running down the wrong road or whether they simply need more tools.

Laura tearfully confessed that she was still recovering from the previous week when she thought she might be pregnant with her third child. She felt that all her hopes and dreams were sliding down the drain as she sat with that serious possibility. She was already busy dealing with two small children and a stressful job. She dreamed of moving up the corporate ladder to be something her dad would be proud of, like a general manager or maybe even a CEO. Her husband worked long hours, so the bulk of the child-rearing and house chores fell squarely on her back. Her mother even commented, "It's a good thing you have a strong back, dear, since everything lands there."

She loved her children dearly. They brought her so much joy but she realized, that she was not a stay-at-home mom. After she was home for over a year with her first child, she was fully ready to go back to work. Laura mentioned that she has such great respect for moms who stay at home full-time and keep their children entertained and well fed. For her, the food situation was a nightly battle. She was too busy to cook and often picked up prepared foods or – even worse – fast food. She always raced to the daycare center, many times arriving just before they closed. She felt guilty about not spending more time with the children and fixing their meals with love.

She was clear that she needed to focus on her career so she could be more independent and better support her family and herself. To her, this was freedom. When she thought child number three was on the way, she felt scared, angry, and trapped. Juggling her job with three children seemed impossible. She was elated when she miscarried, and then berated herself for being a "bad" mom.

Laura loved her husband, John, but ever since the children came along, their relationship had felt distant. He worked long hours to support the family, which she appreciated. She believed there would be time later, after the children were older, to reconnect. She rushed through life much of the time, juggling her responsibilities, and consoled by the fact that he supported her wish to be successful in her career. She wanted not only to progress in her business career but also to stay healthy by exercising regularly while creating a deeper relationship with John and the kids.

Laura was brought up with strong values centered around being educated and being successful in the business world. She never questioned the belief that this was the route to a happier family experience. After all, with her and her husband's hard-earned money, they could take trips to Disneyland or take the children out of the country to bring them joy and expand their horizons.

When Laura's daughter Alyssa started first grade, Laura faced difficult choices. She was bright, but the private school with the best academics had a long waiting list and Alyssa was unlikely to get in that first year. The public school was too easy for her. Laura visited other schools and sat in on their classes. While the Catholic school had a good academic program, it just didn't feel right. The answer to so many questions was, "God made this." While she understood that point of view, she felt it was not the right message for her daughter. Laura went to Catholic school and wanted a different experience for her children. She wanted them to discover their faith in their own way, in an encouraging environment without being told what to believe.

She also visited the Lutheran School, which had a better academic reputation, to experience their teaching style. The way they expressed their beliefs didn't feel right either. She was determined to get Alyssa into the private school so her love for learning was fully nurtured. Since religious teachings or spiritual values were not offered there, those pieces would be totally up to her. That was scary too. She felt unqualified and unsure of her beliefs.

While she wanted her children to feel happy, loved, and accepted, and to have a deep connection to Source, Laura felt helpless there. She couldn't find her connection in her heart to God that she had felt so easily as a child. Without any support from her in this area, her children would be adopting their beliefs from school and the daycare center. Worrying about their inner life was a tall order with everything else on her plate. Laura was afraid they would be left adrift and eventually disconnected from her if she didn't figure this out. She would fail as a mom. She knew were already picking up their values from her and she wondered what they were learning.

Laura didn't feel ready to look too closely at her beliefs. Still, she needed to be that strong, nurturing, spiritual support for her whole family, including herself.

She hadn't discussed this issue with her friends who had small children. She hated to admit that after all her Catholic schooling she felt lost in this area. Her husband was not terribly concerned about this aspect of the children's training. He was more concerned about their academics so they could be successful in the world. This echoed her parent's values. Laura's success hadn't yet brought the happiness she expected. Instead, it brought more striving for that next level of achievement. She was looking for someone she could trust to guide her through.

When she hit this point, Laura could have suppressed her feelings and kept moving forward along the same familiar track. This is the instinctual response, since the mind is programmed to run from pain (or the unknown) and towards pleasure (or in this case, the familiar). To her credit, she took it as a wake-up call, a chance to stop, look at her life, and allow herself to find the joy in living again. She realized that her children not only modeled their behavior after her, but they also took on her beliefs. She is that spiritual leader for her family whether she chooses that, and her interactions with her children will impact their entire life journey. When Laura walked through the doors of FHC, she was relieved to find a place to lay down this burden and receive some training on this aspect of her life.

Awareness Is the First Step

The journey starts with awareness that your habitual response is not working. Most of the time, we are on autopilot, reacting in the way we have been programmed by family, cultural conditioning, or repetition. For example, you might say, "Thank you," as a completely rote response. If you look more closely, many of your other responses are also rote, especially when you are busy or distracted, doing more than one thing at a time. You are missing opportunities to connect, see the bigger picture, or feel what the other person is sitting in.

Instead, you can choose to respond in a more conscious way. If you do, there is an opening for learning some simple techniques to reconnect with your Divine and receive guidance. With practice, you can develop a deep relationship with that inner guidance and access inner stillness no matter what chaos is happening around you. Even while navigating a crowded, noisy room, you can clearly and effectively respond to anyone that interacts with you. This is exactly the skill that can support a busy career mom with two small children and a busy partner. It's too easy in the busyness of life to be pulled off-center, make the wrong decisions and create extra drama and conflict with loved ones. Life starts becoming more alive for us when we can be present to it.

The first step, then, is awareness, and the prerequisite is commitment. Many people shy away from commitments, feeling guilty about their history of unfulfilled agreements. The mind, which is programmed to run from pain, also runs from commitment. It likes to have an escape route and will find a way to keep you from making a solid commitment. If this is true for you, first see how commitment is currently operating in your life, and then consciously decide to commit to this journey. Close off the escape routes. A fulfilling life for you and your family requires you to fully show up. The payoffs are many, and they include healing, peace, empowerment, and productivity.

Along this path, you will meet various aspects of yourself that you may have unconsciously ignored or suppressed. You'll need the warrior who is courageous and focused on the goal. This warrior will persist no matter what. You'll also need your inner child, who is curious and open to learning.

If you have reached a point where your current approach to life is not bringing you that fulfillment, and (perhaps) you have others in your family dependent on you, what will you decide?

Close your eyes. Take three deep, slow breaths and bring your attention to your heart area. Connect with your Divine and repeat these words or something similar that comes to you:

"I am a warrior. I will persist no matter what obstacles appear. I am
a child. I am curious and open to learning and to receiving support.
I commit to my own growth and will do whatever it takes to become
that spiritual leader for my family and community."

Offer gratitude. Open your eyes, smile, and keep breathing.

Chapter 2

WE CAN HELP

Flowering Heart Center

I've actually come across quite a few people with stories similar to Laura's. My heart went out to her, since her story was similar to mine. I remember that moment when I realized I didn't know what I believed or how to guide my children. I knew I had some deep soul searching to do, but there were no books on this topic and I didn't know where to turn. Once I faced these facts and made a commitment to do something about it, various people showed up along the way to guide me. I knew that I could support Laura on her journey to come back into herself; help her find her inner wisdom, strength, and leadership; and support her family in the process.

At a point in my personal journey when I experienced fulfilling relationships and more freedom and joy, I knew I wanted to give back. In 2009, after being initiated at Oneness University to give Oneness Blessings (a transmission of Divine energy), I opened our home to offer group meditations. In 2014, I founded the FHC, a not-for-profit. We welcome everyone there, no matter his or her belief system. Our mission is to create a safe, sacred space for community healing and transformation into higher states of consciousness. In those higher states, the heart opens or flowers.

We have seen people rediscover their faith in themselves and in God (which they may call the Divine, Higher Self, Universe, or Source). I will refer to this intelligent energy as the Divine. Some people experience it in the form of Jesus, Buddha, or Light. Everyone has their own personal journey and relationship with this Divine and watching that unfold is rewarding. We had one Jewish woman take a course with us only to rediscover her love for Jesus. Another Jewish woman during that same time rediscovered her love for her religion and started going back to her temple. While rediscovering this connection may manifest in different ways for everyone, it's always powerful and magical.

Spiritual Leadership

I created a spiritual community around me to support my journey and to keep growing. I thought I knew what it meant to be that spiritual leader for others – leading people through meditations and processes and supporting them through their personal challenges. I learned through my mother's dying process that there are different and equally effective approaches to being that strong, spiritual support. I also realized, to my surprise, that I was a lot like her.

The culmination of my mother's life and all that she was became evident in those last few months, days, hours, and breaths of her life. The quality that struck a chord with me was her deep faith and how she found that inner strength to face her cancer journey with grace, ease, and gratitude. Fiercely self-sufficient throughout her life, she completely surrendered to the process without complaint, offering gratitude to whomever was serving her at the time. I was in awe of her ability to let go at such a deep level.

After she passed, my daughter and I sorted through her personal effects. Besides clothing and a few pieces of jewelry, we mostly found rosaries, holy cards, and medals of various saints. My mother visited the Vatican a several times and attended church every Sunday, even in her later years when it was hard for her to walk. One day, I came across a set of novenas that she had carefully written down – long prayers beseeching God to give her strength, compassion, patience, and love. While holding those slips of paper with her handwriting, I felt a deep pain inside of me, a longing for relief, a sense of helplessness. These prayers were written after my father had passed away. I couldn't imagine the pain my mother experienced after fifty years of marriage and a lifetime of friendship.

There were also prayers in there for other hard times in her life, including the death of my sister. While my mother was clearly that strong, spiritual support for the family in her own way, I had never looked at her as a spiritual leader. These prayers were her private offering, but they had a tremendous effect on all our lives. Everyone in our family has great personal strength, intelligence, wit, and success, and most of us have had a happy home life. Many blessings have run through all our lives. I thought these blessings in my life were the results of my hard work, but my mother laid the foundation. She was a huge support in her way. Today, I gratefully stand on my mother's shoulders and her mother's shoulders, and her mother's mother's.

Your spiritual role within your family won't look like anyone else's. I can support you in creating a vision for yourself of how you would like to be in service. It will evolve over time.

My Personal Journey Begins

I didn't come to this place of leadership within the community easily. To this day, my learning continues. There were critical junctures in my life where I was tested, where I had to reach deep inside to see what I believed, and courageously move forward into unknown territory, facing my fear. Looking back, I see that there was a guide at each turning point to support me through.

When my marriage was on rocky ground and I met my current husband, all that I thought I knew about myself and my life direction changed. I contemplated divorce, but with two small children, it seemed overwhelmingly difficult. When I met Frank, my current husband, I felt as if I had run full-speed into a brick wall. My heart cracked open and all the feelings I repressed for a lifetime spilled out, leaving me scared and confused. In his presence, I spoke my truth for the first time. Some higher force within me took over, because this was not my normal pattern. I had been rushing forward in my life on autopilot, disconnected from my authentic self. Then, when I came to a complete stop and started looking inside, I discovered the guidance I needed was there. It came through loud and clear and compelled me to speak my deepest truth.

I was afraid that Frank would turn his back on me as I revealed what was coming up for me. Before this time, I would never have volunteered to expose myself in this way. One of the truths that I needed to face was that I was not the person of high integrity that everyone thought I was. I was in love with someone else. I knew that I couldn't continue living a lie and that I needed help.

I was led to Dr. Basha Kaplan, a profoundly gifted spiritual clinical psychologist, who guided me through my divorce and the roller coaster ride of emotions I endured over the next three years.

I couldn't have made the journey without her compassion, wisdom and vast experience with this process. Through it all, my interactions with Frank became my own personal growth course. We didn't hold back, and we named where we were sitting each step of the way. Several days a week, we would meet and hold space for each other to speak what we were feeling, where we stood in the relationship and everything else that was happening in our lives. Speaking and listening to that raw truth continued to open my heart. I began to see the connection between truth and love.

Soon after Frank and I moved into a new home and married, my eleven-year-old daughter dropped into a deep depression. I didn't see it coming. She had everything going for her – she was beautiful, smart, witty, and strong. I felt completely helpless in the face of her illness and reached out for help. Although there were no local programs specifically for her age group, I found one that seemed effective. There, I encountered a skilled social worker who helped me navigate my deep guilt around not being there for my daughter. When the private school she attended threatened to expel my daughter because she was getting C's instead of A's, I somehow convinced them that her well-being (staying in school) was much more important than her grades. "Hmm," I thought. "This is interesting. Feeling accepted and good about herself is more important than her academics. What about my well-being versus my success?" I thought success came before happiness. The contemplation began.

I soon had a personal choice to make in this area. I reached a high-level management position at Ameritech and looked at the personal cost of continuing to move up the ladder. My relationship with Frank opened my eyes to the fact that I was not who I thought

I was. Then I took an Artist's Way workshop and started seeing all the ways in which I had lied to myself, and others. I called them "white lies," as if that made them more acceptable. For example, I'd say I was "in a meeting" when I was really out to lunch. When I saw the cost of those lies and how they closed down my heart, I stopped calling them "white lies." I stopped telling lies at work, even when asked to do so by my bosses. I knew if I continued to work in this environment, I would have to veer further away from my true self.

In 1999, I attended a powerful weekend experience for women called, "The Gift – A Rite of Initiation into the Divine Feminine." For the first time, I dropped solidly into my feeling body. Before this experience, I had lived most of my life in my head, analyzing everything. Meeting Frank opened the door to my heart and now I was all the way in, fully embodying myself. The Gift weekend is sponsored by Shematrix. I joined their Mystery School, a collective of women who hold space for others to reach deep within themselves, find their truth, and transform in an expansive field of unconditional love. Their purpose – to ignite global awareness of the mysterious interconnectedness of all life and to cherish each individual as a gateway to infinite possibility – drew me in.

I eventually left my job, and the Shematrix trainers were my trusted guides for the next twenty years. I had much to unlearn from my corporate experience and my strong mind made it even more challenging. I appreciated the patience and support I received from this powerful group to become a more whole and integrated being. I learned to find my voice, express my deepest truth, and hold space for others to do so. This work continues to be my foundation.

In 2008, I found Oneness University in India and started my journey with them of rekindling my faith and deepening my connection to the Divine. In that high-consciousness field, my brain shifted, and I could more easily drop into higher states of consciousness. Their teachings on awakening continue to live in my subconscious and they continue to guide my teachings today. In fact, many of the steps in this book come from this lineage. In 2009, I began to offer meditations at local yoga studios and spiritual centers, and began to gather groups of people in our home to share meditation, Oneness blessings, and teachings.

Because I was overflowing with joy, creativity, and inspiration, I naturally found ways to share these experiences with others. People from all backgrounds, age groups, and belief systems found their way to our door. The intimate groups that formed in our basement grew until we consistently had crowds of fifty people for mediation and blessings. We expanded our offerings, created the not-for-profit FHC, and moved into a commercial space in 2018. The foundation of this center was based not only on the work of Oneness and Shematrix but also on the work of other teachers whose philosophy of openness and wisdom are similar. We've been fortunate to experience the teachings and high-consciousness fields of several enlightened masters at our center. Simply being in their presence shifts people's experience of their lives. FHC honors and meets everyone where they are in life and walks with them on their journeys to reconnect with themselves, their loved ones, and their Divine.

We currently offer weekly meditations, sound healing, and conscious guided movement. Each of these approaches brings people to a deep sense of connection with themselves, embodying Source energy and connecting with others in their lives in a joyful way.

For those who want to take their journey deeper and be a strong support for themselves and others, I also facilitate a series of courses on relationship healing, ancestral liberation, forgiveness, becoming the witness, and relating with the Supreme Consciousness. I have worked with individuals and groups for many years to guide them on their spiritual growth journeys.

I clearly remember my first experience with a somewhat older woman guiding me through my relationship challenges at work. When I asked her how I could ever repay her, she said I couldn't. Simply pay it forward and help whomever needs it. I've endeavored to do just that.

Many community members and personal clients have healed their most challenging relationships and naturally became such a strong support for their families. Some of them reconnected with estranged family and friends. Others created groups and communities of their own. We had high school and college students come to a place of deep acceptance within themselves. In gratitude, a few of them started offering their own meditations in their communities and at their schools. The healings continue to ripple out into the world. One inspiring statement from Sri Bhagavan, founder of Oneness University, is that whenever a family becomes awakened into a high state of consciousness, at least 100,000 people are affected. Focusing on yourself and your family is not only beneficial to you, but it's also in service to all mankind.

This is the work that inspires me. I have been lucky to find skilled guides at each stage of my life journey to be present for my unique process. I can be that guide for you as we venture into this new territory and support you in standing more fully in yourself as a nurturing leader and spiritual support for your family and your community.

Chapter 3

MAP OF THE JOURNEY

Perhaps you feel you've been holding it all together up until now, focusing on your goals and making it all work. Have you noticed that the strategies you've used successfully in the workplace often backfire in your home environment? Try approaching your children like the people who work for you and see how they subvert your attempts at every turn. As you step into that role of boss, your posture, voice, and mannerisms change. Your family notices and, even before you speak, they tune you out.

A similar phenomenon happens internally. Using those workplace strategies in your internal world will likewise wreak havoc, keeping you in a place of comparison and not measuring up to your own ideals. You will be caught in an endless stream of analysis and judgment, spiraling down into a place of contraction and disconnection. Just as your children have asked you to reach deep inside and express what you truly believe, your inner child may now be asking you to do this.

Please know that you are not alone. This book will guide you through a personal journey. Along the way, you will move through fears and obstacles. You will experience a stronger, clearer connection with your inner guidance system and learn to trust it. You can then take action in your life from a more heart-centered place and experience fulfilling relationships in every area of your life. Your life will start to feel less stressful and more magical as you recognize and open to the support that is always there.

The Flowering Heart Process begins with a time out. Our current fast-paced society doesn't appear to be slowing down anytime soon. We see constant deadlines, a steady and relentless barrage of information assailing us from every direction, decisions that need to be made instantly, and music and video broadcasts loudly intruding on us in public places. Our minds are often on the defensive, in the "fight or flight" response mode. It's easy to lose track of what's important and where you want to spend the precious time you're allotted. You might be wasting it looking ahead at some threat down the road, or looking behind with regret, instead of experiencing where you are right now by celebrating your wins and grieving your losses. You may see it in your kids when they are tired and running at full speed. They sometimes become overwhelmed and react with unacceptable behavior, and you might ask them to take a time out to pause and start over. How often do you take that same advice for yourself and pause while experiencing overwhelm?

In this first step of the process, you'll learn a simple technique to slow down and take a brief inventory of the quality of your life in various areas. Then you'll know where to place your focus. In fact, the mere act of putting your attention on your experience begins to shift it.

Step 2 is to ask what you want for your family and your-self. You may be used to setting goals at work or for finances or health conditions. What about deciding how you want your family experience to be or how you want to feel? Back in my busy, less-connected days, I thought this was a useless exercise since I felt I couldn't do anything to fulfill that intention, or perhaps I wasn't ready to do so.

The fact that you are reading this book means you are ready to learn how to set a powerful intention and then follow through. You'll also learn to place your attention on how you are feeling in each moment, whether you feel inspired and uplifted, or whether you are spiraling down into a contracted state. If you are in a con-tracted, disconnected state, you'll realize just how important it is to shift out of that state before relating to others.

Step 3 is to create a deeper relationship with your inner guid-ance system. You might call this your higher self or your Divine. Many of us naturally did this as children. As adults, we get dis-tracted by our thoughts and lose connection with our higher intel-ligence. Seemingly, the more educated people are, the more caught up in their mind they may be, and the harder it might be to detach. We'll look at how you can reliably connect with your higher intelli-gence and foster this relationship in a way that is inspiring for you.

Step 4 is to recognize and move through obstacles. One of the biggest obstacles is carrying pain from your interactions with oth-ers. Even though you may have strong intentions for a loving rela-tionship with your partner, children, and others, the subconscious mind, being much more powerful, holds onto the history of these unresolved hurts. Even seemingly inconsequential ones will con-tinue to create more conflict in your relationships until they are discharged. They also continue to affect your ability to give and receive love and support from others.

Good intentions are not enough here. You need to face the pain from these hurts head-on. Since parents are our first relationship and therefore the blueprint for all relationships, we start there. You might say, "But I have a great relationship with them." That may be true and still you can have many unresolved issues with them from childhood. We'll will explore that one more closely.

Step 5 takes us a little deeper into these relationship hurts. To effectively support your family or your community, you need to be fully accepting of all aspects of yourself and others. There is a difference between condoning behaviors and accepting them. The interesting twist is that when you learn to fully accept and own "bad" behaviors, you'll be less likely to exhibit those behaviors outwardly or be disturbed by them. In fact, you may even learn to love them. This level of acceptance will allow you to respond appropriately and creatively in the face of your children's "misbehavior." You'll begin to see how everything is so interconnected that any work you do with one person or situation positively affects all of your relationships.

In Step 6, you will naturally start to see the bigger picture, leading to a deep inner peace regardless of the outer circumstances. I used to schedule beach vacations in order to find that sense of inner peace. Unfortunately, I found that as soon as I returned home, I needed to schedule the next one, hoping that at least the anticipation would lift my spirits. When I learned to find that place of peace inside, I no longer needed to schedule beach trips.

Seeing the "bigger picture" also brings a sense of gratitude and joy. It takes a commitment to a consistent meditation practice, but once you start feeling the results, you'll want to practice more.

I also recommend that some part of your day be spent in silence. Science is now finding out the importance of silence for the development of your brain. I've heard highly successful business people explain that the less they work, the more money they make. I now understand this seemingly strange concept. It's not that these highly successful people aren't working. Instead, many of them are spending a couple of hours a day in silence. If you can spend at least 20 minutes per day meditating, you will be more acutely tuned into your own inner wisdom and clearer on your priorities for the day. Don't worry if the idea of even taking twenty minutes out of your day sounds daunting. We will start slow here.

Step 7 is to expect miracles. This is a natural outcome of a deep trust and connection with the Divine. Here, you will take that relationship to the next level and allow the grace (Divine influence or favor) that flows to do the heavy lifting. You'll see magic happening all around you and begin to invite it into all of your activities. First you need to let go of your concept of "independence" and, instead, become interdependent with your Divine. It's actually a partnership. If you show up to your part, miracles that your mind can't even grasp will start happening. You will also learn an effective way to pray for what you want for yourself, your loved ones, and your community.

After completing these seven steps, you'll become clear on what it means to you to be that strong, spiritual support for your family or community. I'll show you how to use what you have learned to show up for others in a powerful way. You'll also get a sense of the importance of community. You can't always see what is happening for you, so fellow travelers on the journey with you are essential here.

You'll ultimately realize and have huge gratitude for the fact that you are a strong guide for your family. With your newfound inner freedom, the desire to give back to your family and community will naturally be there. You'll experience wonder, amazement, and awe at the world around you and feel more alive and present to everyday life. Remember, you probably experienced this state as a child. Let's bring that back.

The best way to use this book is to go through the chapters in order. Spend as much time with each one as you like. When you have completed all the steps, use it as a reference book and revisit to the chapters you feel you need to do the most work on. Remember that obstacles will appear along the way. These don't mean that you are doing anything wrong. In fact, generally we receive at least three challenges just before we take a leap in our growth. Some people get discouraged, thinking they are going backwards, and so they often stop when, in fact, success is just around the corner. There is a catch, though. You can't be "reaching" for success or you will have already lost the present moment. Accepting where you are now is important. Use the processes in this book to embrace your current circumstances. Persevere through the inevitable challenges and experience more freedom, clarity, and empowerment. Keep persisting. Help is always available for those who are smart enough and humble enough to ask.

Take a deep breath, ask yourself if you are ready, and then turn the page.

Chapter 4

TIME OUT!

This Flowering Heart Process begins with the seemingly simple step of stopping and looking at where you are right now. It requires a full stop. Then, look at all that you are juggling and prioritize where to put your time and attention now. Don't wait for a time where you are juggling less. Contemplate on the different areas of life and where you would like to improve. Your current experience is the result of unconscious patterns that have been running your life. Bringing consciousness or awareness there will shift your experience.

You can't get from New York to Washington, D.C., if you are sitting in Chicago. You might feel like you are rushing all the time. It's almost painful to come to a full stop. Why is that? Why do we put children in time out? Why don't we put ourselves in time out?

You children now challenge you to "get real" about where you stand in your life and what you believe in. But you may only know the act of running. Since you are consistently looking down the road, you may think that you are further along than you actually are. As a result, you might think you are in New York rather than Chicago. Any plan you create from this place is headed for failure.

I have seen this often with clients who believe their relationship with their spouse is fine because they haven't had a major argument in the last few months. They rarely communicate about how they feel or what is going on for them inside. Their conversations revolve around the schedule, handling the household issues, or what happened at work. In Laura's case, she was afraid of what she would find if she really looked at the current health of this relationship. This process of pretending that all is well and charging forward is a common strategy. To create the quality of life you are looking for, you need to tap into your inner warrior and be willing to see.

Rushing through life is an escape because we are uncomfortable standing still. To stand still means we have to look at who we are and feel what is happening in our life in this moment. We might prefer to be in New York, but that is a fantasy. If we are always rushing, we don't take the time to look inward and see what's true for us.

There are plenty of apparently compelling reasons to keep rushing ahead: deadlines, meetings, chores, responsibilities – the list is endless. The temptation is to go faster to get more done. At work, you might be chasing after more success. At home, you might be rushing to get your children to after-school activities and to put food on the table.

I often hear people say that when they are good enough at their job, when they have been recognized as successful and awarded a big salary, things will ease up for them and their families. They imagine hiring a gardener, chef, or personal secretary so they can slow down and do things they enjoy. Instead, they immediately fill their "extra" time with a long list of other activities. It may be a more enticing list, like working out or getting a massage, but they will have a very full schedule and still be running. The scenery may be better, but, believe me, the experience is not.

The point is that you have a certain capacity, a certain number of plates that you can keep spinning at once. If you drop one or choose to put it down, you reflexively pick up another. The idea of, "When I have time, then I will slow down and take stock of my life and decide what I want," is false. There is no such time, unless you wait until you are forced into it by illness or other unexpected events. Your calendar may look clear a few months down the road, but by the time you get there, it will be full too. It's not the number of plates you are spinning, it's a matter of priority. We can simply decide to stop running.

I used to wake up with a list of to-dos scrolling through my head. I jumped out of bed and checked items off the list before I stepped into the shower. The more tasks I completed before I walked out the door to work, the prouder I was of myself. Later, when I became more conscious about what was really going on, I realized some of those chores didn't need to get done (e.g., taking out the trash – just before the cleaning lady arrives) and other ones needed to be redone later because my focus had been on completion rather than the important details of the work.

Now I start my day with a time out. I wake up and sit still for fifteen to twenty minutes listening to a guided meditation or simply watching my mind. When I feel complete with this, I tune into what is most important for me to put my attention on that day. Invariably, my inner guidance is right on. Those fifteen to twenty minutes in the morning probably save me at least 30 to 45 minutes of frantic, wasted effort.

What I love about the expression "time out" is that I see it as stepping out of time. The mind, when it is based in time, is usually living in the past or in fear of the future. When I take a time out, I am consciously stepping out of that mind space into a timeless space.

Time Out

The first step when confronted by your children or by other life circumstances that demand something more substantive from you is to stop rushing. The first step is not a step at all. It's a full stop. Tune into your breathing and let it bring you more present. Your breathing in a stressful state is likely short and shallow, which is normal for an active mind. To slow down the mind and sync with the body, begin slowing down your breath. Take three deep, slow breaths and bring as much of your focus to the breathing process as possible. This is a time out to reconnect with yourself.

The seemingly simple, but startling question: "What do I believe?" requires a conscious reconnection inside. It requires you to slow down and be in the present moment. If you try to "think it through," the mind will give you beliefs from your past that were probably given to you by other people: parents, schoolteachers, priests, et cetera. Or the mind will go into the future and find even more fearful beliefs. "If you don't put your children in a Catholic School, they won't learn any values and you will suffer the consequences later." You're being asked to let go of those past or future thoughts, reach deeper inside and discover what's true for you now. It will be revealed if you just keep focusing on your breath.

The hardest part about this simple approach is that is goes against all of your previous wiring. Success at your job may require using your knowledge and problem-solving skills, and you've been trained through many years of schooling to do just that. You are an expert at actively engaging your mind and applying it to whatever task is before you. It may seem logical to use that well-honed skill to deal with this question – "What do I believe? Let me think about that." Immediately, back you go into the past or the future. Breathe; let go.

The fact that you realize you don't know what you believe is actually great news. It means you are ready and open for learning. Many of our biggest obstacles arise from thinking we know and plowing forward. The fact that you are reading this book means you are reaching out for help. A willingness to sit with not knowing and to ask for help are two important prerequisites for this journey.

Let's explore.

Quality of Life Inventory

You'll start with a pen and paper exercise and then work your way deeper inside. Take just a few minutes with this short inventory of certain areas in your life, noticing where you stand with them. This will give you some insight into these aspects of your current reality:

- Family Relationships
- Work Relationships
- Personal Fulfillment
- Spiritual Connection
- Contribution to Your Community or to Society

First, rate your quality of life in each of the categories above from one to five, where five is the highest quality. Do this quickly without thinking too much. Second, rank these areas in importance to you, from one to five. Third, estimate the percentage of your time that you spend in each area. When you are complete with these steps, close your eyes and take a deep breath. Find your inner child who is curious and open to learning. Now, open your eyes and look at the results.

What do you notice? Most people experience a low quality of life in the areas in which they spend the most time. While family relationships may be a high priority, you might spend less of your time interacting with them than you would like. However, if the quality of time is high, it doesn't need to be a high percentage of your overall time.

Take a moment and think about a time when your parent or spouse deeply listened to your concerns. How did that impact you? It may have been a defining moment for you. I remember a time in sixth grade that I brought home a math test with an F for my mom to sign. It was unusual for me to get a low grade, so this was a new experience, and I was terrified to hand it to her. She looked at the paper, laughed out loud, and then gave me a hug. In that moment, I understood that the F did not define me. I felt seen and acknowledged. You'll find that you can easily recall moments like this one because they are so powerful they can literally nourish you for a long time. These deeply touching moments feed us on a deep level, meeting our core need to receive love.

This inventory shows what you value and what areas of your life may need more attention so your life experience can be more enjoyable. If your life seems too busy, you may find you allot a small percentage of your time to contributing to others. If so, that simply means you are operating from a deficit. When you feel fulfilled, you naturally give back regardless of your schedule. Again, it's *important* not to judge, but just to see the truth.

Much of your current experience in all of these areas is likely based on some old patterns and behaviors that you learned early in life. Instead of chasing the solutions outside of you, this part of the journey takes you inside, where the deeper wisdom lies. If you are looking for the answers "out there," you can be pulled off center.

Now that you've experienced the importance of placing yourself in time out, and you've become aware of your current reality, you can choose to place your attention and focus on what it is that you really want.

Next, we'll look at the experience you might prefer.

Chapter 5

WHAT DO I WANT?

You might be used to setting goals in your work life and perhaps you have some personal goals around finances or health, but have you ever stopped to look at your intention for your family's well-being? What is your deepest wish for your children, and for your relationship with them and with your spouse? Armed with knowledge of the truth, you can consciously decide on and set a powerful intention. An intention is a goal or a desire that you feel strongly about. We have "desires" all day long which may be fleeting or easily satisfied. An intention, on the other hand, takes real attention, focus, and passion. Because of this, you'll likely have the energy for only a handful of intentions at a time.

You may not have realized that you can effectively set intentions around feeling happy and fulfilled in a relationship. If you don't, you are at the effect of whatever old patterns and beliefs are operating in your consciousness. You will keep getting more of the same. I'm reminded of a quote from *Alice in Wonderland*:

"Would you tell me, please, which way I ought to go from here?"
"That depends a good deal on where you want to get to."
"I don't much care where —"
"Then it doesn't matter which way you go."

Not setting an intention for yourself means you don't care where you are going. If you are still with me here, I'm guessing you do care.

There was a time I didn't realize I could make intentions around feeling happy or loved. It either happened or it didn't. Since this goal didn't have specific milestones I could work toward, what use was it? I preferred to focus on measurable goals I could accomplish. Looking back at this now, it's amusing, but it wasn't then. Because I wasn't intentional in this area, I was affected by the whims of the world around me. I came face-to-face with this in my relationship with my current husband, Frank. We were deeply in love and both clear that this was the relationship we had both been seeking. He was in the midst of leaving his wife. I was separated from my husband and anxiously awaiting a time where I could be together with Frank. But he had a lot of internal work to do before he was ready to move forward, and I watched helplessly from the sidelines.

From my point of view, he had done nothing to work towards his goal of being with me. There were no external clues, no measurable steps he took. One day, I got the courage to ask him what his milestones were, and he burst out laughing. "What milestones? I just wade in and figure it out."

I was shocked. How do you operate without a series of steps to reach a goal? That didn't compute in my world, but I was also relieved. From my point of view, he wasn't even on step one. From his point of view, he could be anywhere along the path. My goal was to be together and I was looking for external, measurable progress points. His goal was to leave with as much integrity as possible and to make sure he did all he could in the situation. How do you measure that? Similarly, if you make a goal around happiness, how do you measure that? This was how my mind operated at that time.

Take a look at this possibility of setting a course toward where you want to go in your relationships. In the previous chapter, you looked at the quality of your relationships and got a high-level sense for where they are right now. They are in their current states because of certain patterns, beliefs and habitual behaviors. Once we become aware of these, we can shift them. The first step is to look more deeply into your current reality.

Current Reality Contemplation

Start by closing your eyes and taking three deep breaths.

Bring the faces of your children before you and look into their eyes.

Feel that connection. Breathe.

Now look at your experience with them over the past few days.

Observe your interactions without judgment and from a place of curiosity.

What do you notice?

Sit for a few minutes here until you feel complete.

Bless your children.

Breathe and release them.

Take another deep slow breath.

Bring the image of your partner before you and look into his or her eyes.

Breathe. Feel your connection.

Observe your interactions over the last few days without judgment.

Keep breathing deeply.

What do you notice?

Sit for a few minutes here until you feel complete.

Bless your partner and then release.

Take another deep slow breath.

Breathe in forgiveness for yourself.

Breathe out whatever you are holding onto from the process.

Open your eyes.

Take a few minutes to write any insights in your journal.

What did you notice during this process? Was there a lack of connection in some of your interactions? While you were talking with them, were you also thinking about what else you needed to do? If so, know that this is completely normal, and the way much of our society operates right now. Maybe, instead, you had many moments of relating from a place of pure presence and deep connection.

Either way, you can create a vision for how you would like to experience the day-to-day interactions with your family and set a powerful intention. Experience tells us that every effective leader has a vision for what they want to create, and then they put energy behind it. How the vision unfolds is many times a mystery, especially when there are no milestones for you to measure. It works, nonetheless.

Creating the Reality You Prefer

You've realized that your children's well-being is up to you. You and your partner can decide which school they attend and therefore what beliefs they may encounter in that learning environment.

Ultimately, they pick up their primary values and beliefs from you and your partner; in fact, they already have. Now that you are conscious about your leadership role here and the current state of affairs, you can decide what you would like to support them in becoming. You can decide how you would like to experience your family.

Instructions

The worksheet below will support you in writing an intention. The ideas included are suggestions. If you prefer to create your own, you are welcome to do so. If you do, make sure they are in present tense. Before you start writing, bring yourself fully present. Close your eyes and take three deep, slow breaths. Bring your focus into your heart. See your family there and feel the joy of that connection, then open your eyes and start writing.

Worksheet

Fill in the sentence with the first words that come to mind.

I want my children to feel (happy, loved, inspired) _____.

Or, I want my children to be (happy, creative, loving) _____.

I want my relationship with my children to be (playful) _____.

I want my relationship with my partner to be _____.

Now that you are clear of what you would like for your family, you can word the intentions in a way where you take responsibility for your piece of it.

Now we can look at the intentions we would like to hold and bring it back to ourselves. For example, I may want my children to feel happy, so my intention is to support them in being that. That is my leadership role here.

I create a space where my children feel _____.

Or I support my children in being _____.
My relationship with my children is _____.
My relationship with my partner is _____.
My life is _____.

When you have completed this process, keep these written statements somewhere you will see them on a daily basis.

This will help to keep your focus on this area, and you'll start to respond differently to life situations.

These intentions are heart-based, and they come from a desire of wanting closer connections with the family. You might feel inspired simply by reading them.

Let's look at the intention Laura set for herself around the issue that precipitated this whole journey for her – her daughter's schooling.

She already knew which school she wanted. If she didn't, she could have created an intention for Alyssa to get into the school that would serve her best in her life journey. Either intention would have been fine. She could also get input from her daughter and include what she wants in the intention. In this case, Laura was clear she wanted the private school, and she set the following intention.

"I do what it takes to get Alyssa into Roycemore school by Fall 2015."

In this example, Laura had an active role to play in supporting this intention. Once she wrote it down and focused on it, she became clear on her next action steps to make this happen. This is a key step. Nothing would have happened for her if she had not taken action. She listened to her intuition and talked with the principal. After a series of conversations, Alyssa was invited into the school. That last step was the result of grace flowing into the situation.

I learned a valuable formula at Oneness University in India:

Growth = Intention + Effort + Grace.

Once you set the intention, you must do everything in your power to support it. Only then will grace flow in, create the synchronicities, and bring you resources that you need. We will talk more about that component later.

Since Laura's other concern was about Alyssa's value system in a school where there were no religion classes, she added another intention.

"I effectively guide my daughter through her grade school years in a way that instills self-love and acceptance, and supports a deep and powerful relationship with her Divine."

Take time to get still, breathe and connect in your heart before writing out your intentions. Don't worry about whether you've included absolutely everything or if they are perfect. They can serve as a starting point and you can revisit them as you get clearer about what you want. Regardless of where you are, it's important to have intentions and write them down. Check in periodically with yourself to see if they continue to feel inspiring to you. Take action and allow the process to unfold.

I had a strong intention to sell our home last year. Everyone was praying for it, including several monks in India. Although I wanted to sell, the urgency came from a place of desperation. The property taxes were high, and we couldn't support the costs of ownership any longer. Furthermore, I hadn't even looked for places for us to live. I was in total fear around our future and afraid of going into foreclosure on the property. I couldn't understand why the intention didn't work.

Later, I realized that the Universe had better plans. My mother's health was rapidly declining, and I needed to be totally focused on her. Had we sold that house when I intended, dealing with both the move and my mom would likely have been too much. Also, when my mom passed, some life insurance money came through quickly and I was able to pay the outstanding bills, do the necessary repairs to make selling our home easier, and update her place for us to eventually live there. Now, we are setting a new intention for selling our home, and it's sourced from a place of inspiration and joy. I expect it will sell soon.

Looking at whether each specific intention is originating from a place of joy or fear is important. Many times, people set goals out of competition and comparison. Years ago, I created a strong intention to become a general manager at my company. That intention was sourced from competition. Both of my siblings were successful lawyers and my dad was a successful businessman, so I hoped to gain his approval this way. While I became a general manager through a lot of hard work, it was not a fulfilling experience for me. I left the company within a few years of reaching that goal.

Had I been more conscious and tuned-in when I set that goal, I would have realized it wasn't inspiring me. I may have also seen that it was coming from a place of competition with my family and might have been motivated to set an entirely different intention. When our intentions are sourced from a place of inspiration, not only will the goal be fulfilling, but also the entire journey will be rewarding. This has been my experience with the creation of the FHC. Whatever intention you choose to set, make sure it is coming from a place of love and inspiration rather than fear, jealousy, revenge, or competition.

We've looked at two types of intentions to support what you want for yourself and your family. One is an experience of how you want it to feel and another is a goal you want to accomplish. One is more passive (how it feels) and the other is more active (requiring effort on your part). There is a different kind of effort required in creating the more passive, feeling-based intentions, and we will develop those skills later in the chapter on relationships.

Now that you are clear on what you want, and that it comes from a place of inspiration and you're committed to put in the required effort, there is room for grace to flow. That's the game-changer. This is where synchronicities and miracles show up. To allow this to happen, you will need to strengthen your relationship with Spirit.

Chapter 6

CONNECT WITH THE EXPERTS

Your inner guidance system is critical to your success in being a strong support for your family or community. You will need to take a look at this relationship with yourself and create it in a way that inspires you to stay connected. We will look at the consequences of operating from a disconnected state and then give you a reliable way to reconnect. Then it's up to you to stay aware of when you are connected or disconnected. This is key to operating from a place of harmony and supporting others versus conflict and separation.

I've had quite the journey with God/Spirit/the Divine/Universe/Source. I've had such difficult relationships here that only recently have I felt safe to use the word "God." For me, it was associated with an old man in the sky who rebukes anyone who transgresses his commandments. He is there to keep the law of the land. Of course, both of my siblings are lawyers, so this is definitely one lens I see the world through. God was scary to me as a young child, especially when I had to go to confession in a dark booth, enumerating my sins (or making some up since I couldn't remember) and receiving my "punishment" in the form of prayers. This is how it seemed to me through the eyes of my second grader. I had a strategy – hide! So I did.

I figured God was busy with lots of other people and wouldn't notice. In my teenage years, I shifted from hiding to rebellion. I rebelled against God and authority in all forms, in my own more quiet, sneaky way. While the male authority in the church was cold and distant, the female authority figure seemed absent and disempowered. There was no one to turn to. When I was married in the Church, I left out the ritual of offering flowers to Mary because I didn't feel her presence. Later, I couldn't deny there was magic happening in my life, so I tentatively admitted there was a Divine hand operating. I preferred to call it "Source" or the "Universe." I wanted to keep it vague and a little distant since it still seemed to hold a dangerous power.

As I stepped more fully into the world of service and personal growth, I started consciously reaching out to connect with "Spirit," which was more of a light energy with little personality. Since being in the Shematrix mystery school, I started connecting more powerfully with the Divine Feminine, which goes by many names: the mystery, the Big She, the circle around the yin and the yang, the void, etc. I came to appreciate Mary's power and returned her to a place of honor in my soul. I realized the Divine Feminine energy was so powerful that others sought to diminish or eradicate it. It was not until I attended the Oneness University that I was able to reconnect with my original form of "God," not from a place of fear and punishment but as something more relatable and friendly. I returned the male aspects of God to a place of honor in my heart.

I finally understood God was who I created Him or Her to be and I could create the relationship I desired.

Since I had my own personal God, I didn't have to wait in line with my requests, or wait for an issue worthy of Divine help. My relationship deepened tremendously and the fear that kept me away from the Divine evaporated. I became open to receiving help for everything: finding parking spaces, going grocery shopping, and reaching out to others. Then I remembered that I actually felt this way as a very young child. Now the Divine appears in my heart most often as light, but it can also show up as Jesus or Mary or several other forms.

Everyone's belief system is personal and heavily influenced by family and cultural experiences. The type of relationship you have with your personal Divine is usually based on your primary relationships: parent, teacher, partner, or friend. It is subject to the same difficulties and conflicts you experience in those relationships. We will work on that in the next chapter. For now, let's reconnect and get a sense of who the Divine is for you and how it operates in your life.

First, find a quiet space where you won't be disturbed, lay down, and relax.

Divine Relationship Process

Take three deep slow breaths.

Go back to your childhood, to your earliest memories of being connected to the Divine.

Bring an image before you of the form your Divine took then. It could be an image or a feeling.

What was your relationship? Did God listen to you?

What comes up for you when you look at this image now?

What judgments, opinions, and beliefs do you have about this image?

Relax and be aware of these – there's no need to do anything.

Who is projecting these beliefs onto this image?

This is an aspect of the Divine, one that is operating in your consciousness.

Look into the eyes (if there is an image) and acknowledge this one.

Move forward in time to school age when you were indoctrinated into a religion, went to church or a synagogue, or were told what to believe about God.

What image or form did your Divine take then?

What was your relationship to it?

Now, as an adult looking at this image, what feelings does it evoke?

What judgments, opinions, and beliefs do you have about this image?

Relax and just be aware of these – you don't need to do anything.

Who is projecting these beliefs onto this image?

This is an aspect of the Divine, one that is operating in your consciousness.

Look into the eyes (if there is an image). Make peace with this one.

Move forward in time again. See if the Divine took on any other forms for you.

Are there images that have come to you, but you resisted them because they challenged your belief systems or didn't fit into your idea of the Divine?

Take a moment and explore. Do a scan.

Invite any old, rejected, or dismissed images to arise.

Maybe you were Catholic and the image that appeared to you was Muslim or Pagan.

Maybe you were Jewish and Jesus appeared.

Take a moment and see if there are images you disowned.

This too is an aspect of the Divine. Look into the eyes of this one and make peace with it.

As long as you are resisting an image of the Divine, you are creating this push/pull relationship.

Notice all the opinions, beliefs, and ideas you have associated with various images of the Divine. Where did those come from?

They have worn whatever projections you have given them.

The Divine will willingly take on any form that you give it.

You can choose the one you have or create a new form.

What is your relationship with your Divine currently?

Does He or She give you what you want?

Is He /She punishing? Do you have to ask multiple times to get an answer?

God will relate to you in the way that you want.

You have created this relationship unconsciously until now, based on the collective beliefs or what you learned in school.

Now, create a Divine who is powerful enough to fulfill your desires.

If you relate to a Divine that is powerful, playful, and attentive, then that will be your experience. If you say He is indefinable, that's your experience. If She is punishing or indifferent, then that will be your experience. You can choose to have a punishing God or a playful God.

Which do you want?

As you design this one, make it someone you can relate to.

What image works for you? Is it a man, a woman, or simply light?

Examine your image for a few minutes, filling in any details you wish.

Now, consciously design the type of relationship you choose.

Do you want to relate to the Divine as your friend, your mother, your sibling, or your partner?

How does your Divine respond to you?

Does He / She anticipate your needs?

Is He/ She powerful enough to give you what you desire?

Do you have to work for it?

What is their personality like? Playful? Humorous? Serene? Inviting? Easy to talk to?

Take a few minutes to experience this Divine in the way you designed.

Take some time to record in a journal what you discovered in this process. Also, to make room for your inner child to come out, markers or crayons may be helpful. If your Divine has a form than draw the image. List the characteristics and how you want the Divine to relate to you. Notice if there were any surprises for you. I've seen people shocked to see their Divine appear in the form of a different faith than the one they practiced. It was also very freeing for them to see that and to choose the form they prefer to experience.

There are a couple of important points to note about this relationship you are designing. The Divine will relate to you in the way you relate to it. If you want a playful connection, you'll have to connect playfully. The Divine also relates to you in the way you relate to others in your life. Again, if you want a playful connection, bring that quality into your other relationships.

Once you are clear on the form and relationship, take some time to relate to your Divine by having a conversation. You may have naturally done this as a child. Start with two minutes. Then, whenever you remember throughout the day, connect in. When you notice your mind talking to itself about something that happened yesterday or a fear about the future, stop and talk to your Divine instead. You'll feel an immediate shift in energy from density to lightness. The minute you turn your attention to the Divine, They're there for you. If you don't feel that presence, there are many ways to reconnect. The most reliable way is with speaking your truth.

Truth

Connecting with the Divine is like connecting with a giant field of love. Being authentic opens our hearts so we can experience that love. So much of the time, and in many interactions, we may be trying to conform to an image that we hold of ourselves. Even with the Divine, we might put on a good self-image so that we appear worthy of receiving help. Then the mind naturally looks for supporting evidence that we are that kind, smart, or loving person.

The reason the mind has to scramble for evidence to support this "good" self-image is that we are not actually feeling that way. It's not, in fact, the truth. One quick way to reconnect is to speak what's true for you right now. For example, you might honestly say, "I am feeling disconnected, unworthy, unlovable." You might truthfully say, "I need support so I can look good and get approval from my boss or my partner."

The Divine has no judgment and, in fact, is aware of all of this. By speaking the truth, we become more humble and open to receiving. The mind quiets and the Presence is much stronger. In my experience, truth and love are two sides of the same coin. For this reason, a reliable way to reconnect or stay connected to your inner guidance is to be brutally honest with yourself in every moment. You don't have to speak that out loud – just speak it inside and watch what happens.

Barbara came to FHC many years ago looking for relief from her relentless judgmental thoughts. She was disconnected from her family and in chronic pain from a knee replacement surgery. After setting intentions, connecting with her Divine, and working with me through some challenging family relationship issues, she was able to see and release her judgments. Her pain would disappear during these sessions when she was seeing and not attaching to those stressful thoughts. As she continued the work, she noticed that her pain practically disappeared every time she was honest with herself and connected with the Divine. Now, when her knee pain returns, she knows it's time to do another level of introspection and she comes to FHC. While she can do some of this on her own, she finds it easier in a small group setting with other community members.

There are many benefits to maintaining this connection. Not only will your intentions be readily fulfilled, but also you will also receive the guidance you need to navigate life in a more powerful way. Decisions, such as which school to place your children in, will be clearer. What you may need to do today to support your kids so they can feel happier will become clearer. As this inner relationship deepens and you learn to trust it more, life becomes more magical. This connection is vital to living a fulfilling and happy life.

Guidance

I often get the question, "How do I know whether my guidance is coming from my higher self or from my ego?"

You are developing a relationship with the Divine through more awareness and ongoing conversation. With experience, you'll get a sense of what communication or guidance from your Divine feels like. Some people actually hear the words. Others experience a gut feeling or a knowing, or see visions. One of our community members asks for guidance about which food to pick in the grocery store. She knows which fruit to pick when looking at the entire bin of oranges because one or two will appear brighter and shinier than the others. Similarly, she scans the shelves for any food that pops out at her. This is how her guidance is received in that aspect of her life.

As you relate to your Divine, you will discover how you receive the information most clearly. If it's a decision, you'll notice the choice that feels lighter is usually the correct one. You can also ask for a sign that you've chosen correctly. Be alert to animals or birds that cross your path, billboards, and messages from others. Offer gratitude to your Divine for that guidance. This step is important because it builds relationship. This is a learning process, so take notes. Notice when you ignore a message from your Divine and see what consequences arise. I see this happening periodically with small decisions or actions. Recently, I missed my cue and got locked out of the house, then I thanked my Divine for trying to warn me. Sometimes, I might apologize to my Divine for consciously not following a direction I received. Many times, I'll ask my Divine to keep talking to me and to perhaps speak louder especially when I appear not to listen. Relate, communicate, and offer gratitude to build this connection. It's important to bring awareness to when your connection has dropped and you are flying solo. This can lead to difficulties.

Disconnection versus Connection

When we are disconnected, we are often caught up in the conflict that is happening in our minds. The mind is positional, with opinions about everything. This is because the mind is basically a measurement tool. Comparison is the way it measures whether something is "good" or "bad" and whether there is a potential threat to our existence. The mind is constantly searching the horizon for some hazard lurking there. While we are rarely exposed to a situation that can cause us bodily harm, we are often in psychological danger – worrying about our finances, health, or relationships. The mind doesn't know the difference between real physical danger and imagined, psychological threats – it's simply trying to protect us. The mind becomes very agitated in facing any type of danger and it threatens gloom and doom. A state of disconnection is where you are caught up in these thoughts or in a lower state of consciousness. In this state, any decision you make or any action you take will cause more disturbance or conflict. Yogi Bhajan said it simply and powerfully: "Every sequence (action or thought) creates a consequence."

Think about the times you snapped at your partner or your kids when you were upset about something that happened at work or with your friend. The guilt you probably felt afterwards for hurting them made it worse. You might then have been tempted to lash out at someone or to send that snappy email to a friend who said something slightly off to you. If you give into these thoughts, you find yourself spiraling down into a denser and more contracted state. Your heart closes. That's why it's so important to be aware that you are upset and stop before you pick up the phone, send that text, or fire off that email. Taking that step will simply escalate the disturbance, creating more pain for you. Some of the community members at FHC have explained to me that when they start to text from a place of being disturbed, my voice appears in their head saying, "Don't send that text!" They are then grateful to have avoided another dose of pain.

Any decisions you make from a disconnected state will also result in more conflict in your life at some point down the road. Remember when we looked at the source of your intentions to make sure that they were from an inspired state rather than a lower state of consciousness? I experienced this in college when I had a fight with my boyfriend. He asked me right after the fight if he could borrow my car. My guidance was screaming no, but I said yes, afraid that otherwise he would disappear for a long time. He left, still upset, drove the car into town and ran into a pole by the train tracks. When he came back to my room to tell me that he totaled the car, I was angry and also terrified he might have injured other people. I didn't want that responsibility on my hands. (Thankfully, no one was injured.)

Disturbances inside create disturbances outside. Watch and see for yourself.

Take a few moments to contemplate this.

Disconnection Contemplation

Close your eyes and take three deep, slow breaths.

Connect in the heart with your Divine.

Ask to be shown where you have made decisions from this place of conflict, and the resulting sequence of events that occurred afterwards.

Relax and allow yourself to be shown what you need to see.

When you feel complete, open your eyes and write down any insights.

Noticing the disconnection is often enough to come back into connection. You can tell your Divine how you feel and ask for help. I sometimes chant mantras to bring myself back into alignment. Since I know that every sequence creates consequences, I prefer to work on generating positive sequences whenever possible. One effective way to do this is chanting internally or externally using powerful Sanskrit phrases. Since many of these phrases have been chanted for thousands of years, they have created a deep groove in consciousness and your mind will readily follow down those positive tracks, repeating the phrases long after you stop.

There are many beautiful chants with different purposes available on YouTube. My favorites are the Moola Mantra (often called the telephone to God) and the Ganesha Mantra (to remove obstacles). If this approach appeals to you, find a chant that speaks to you and chant it 7, 21, 49, or 108 times every day. You can use a mala to keep track of the number of chants. Alternatively, If you prefer, you can use a rosary and say the appropriate prayers. After practicing these mantras or prayers for sometime, you may notice that when your mind is idle, it starts chanting something positive rather than generating negative sequences through thoughts of comparison and judgment. This will keep you in an inspired and connected state.

It's vital to be aware of when you are connected and when you are disconnected. The quality of your life experience depends on it. There is no middle ground. Either you drop down into a contracted state or you feel connected, uplifted, expansive, and in harmony with your surroundings. Keep your attention on what state you are in. Keep speaking to your Divine to keep that connection open.

Take action toward your intentions and make decisions from a place of connection with the Divine and your life will become magical. Just remember that you are not alone. When you hit a place of uncertainty, connect. Ask. Listen. Take the Divine along with you for the whole journey, not just when you need help.

Start becoming aware as often as you can throughout the day. Are you connected or disconnected? In my small groups, people report back that they are initially surprised by how often they are disconnected. They have done a lot of personal work and yet they see how disconnected they are much of the time. I'm always excited to hear this because it shows that they are becoming more aware. The mere act of seeing it will be enough. People in this group have created such strong connections with their Divine that their other relationships start healing. It seems miraculous but, in fact, it's inevitable. All of our relationships are interconnected.

Now that we have more awareness and know how to reconnect, let's look at little more deeply at the root causes of disconnection.

Chapter 7

OBSTACLE COURSE

"Our Quality of life depends on the quality of our relationships."
~ *Sri Amma Bhagavan* ~

You want a loving relationship with your kids and your partner? Paradoxically, the path to those relationships starts with healing your primary relationships, those with your parents. Because this relationship is our first experience it is the blueprints for all other relationships. Generally, we model our style after our parents or in resistance to them. To step out of this dynamic and find our own path, we need to release the charges that keep us tied into it. Setting these relationships right will cascade into all others. You'll begin by noticing the filters you see them through and use different viewpoints to loosen your hardened perceptions. We will then take a close look at the partner relationship and see what you can learn about yourself. Finally, we will look at how relationships backslide or fail, and what to do to bring back the beautiful connection.

Look back again at your inventory of the quality of your family and work relationships. There is likely to be at least one challenging one. If it's a work relationship, you might think, "That's okay. I only deal with him occasionally." That challenging relationship is actually showing where you need to focus. It's not possible to cut that person out of your life and expect the tension to be gone. It will simply reappear in your relationship with someone else. These challenges reflect your feelings about an area of relationships in which you have struggles. Perhaps the behavior they exhibit is something you are not owning in yourself, because the mind is quick to blame the other rather than look inside.

It's easier to face this current challenge when you recognize it rather than ignoring it and encountering a louder version later. The more you suppress unpleasant interactions, the larger those disturbances become in your consciousness. Since the Universe is conspiring in your favor to heal this issue, it will simply bring you someone else with similar characteristics. In fact, the next one to appear will have more energy behind it because the hurt is growing larger. Instead of ignoring a relationship issue when it arises, it's more useful to simply get curious and ask what it is bringing up in you.

When I first began to look at my relationships this way, I was skeptical. At the time, I thought my mother was highly critical and, believe me, I had gathered plenty of evidence. As I blamed her, other people in my life seemed to be more critical, too. When I finally looked inside, saw my strong inner critic, and embraced that quality, my mother actually stopped being critical of me. I was in disbelief and kept looking for it to show up in her again. It never did. The disturbance I was carrying in my system around being criticized had been fully experienced and released from my system. It no longer activated her critical personality.

Even though your most challenging relationship may be a friend, co-worker, or ex-partner, you'll start by working on your relationships with your parents. They are your first relationships, even experienced through gestation in the womb. Your consciousness was taking it all in even though you weren't fully formed. Even if your mother or father wasn't around much during your early years, their imprint is still there. Your other guardians would also have a big impact if they took care of you during the first six years of your life.

Sri Bhagavan teaches that your life script is written within the first six hours after your birth. The first six years of life, before your rational brain forms, is also an impactful time. You are an emotional being, and how you were treated or accepted, and the beliefs you took on during this time also have a big impact on your life. The programs and conditioning from this time lies deep within your unconscious. It influences your day-to-day experience and how you react to life situations. Your life is run by these programs operating in your unconscious. Bringing awareness to these programs will loosen their power.

If you look deeply, you might notice that you are modeling your own parenting either after your parents or in resistance to their approach. Either way, your parenting is arising out of a subconscious pattern. Take a look at your relationship with your children and see where this may be true. I tried hard to do it differently than my mom. I consciously tried not to be like her. It wasn't until she died and I was going through her personal effects that I started to realize that I was a lot like her. It broke my heart to realize

I hadn't seen this sooner. The image I held was from my teenage years when I felt distant from her and full of judgments. While I worked hard on that relationship and eventually developed a closeness with her, I didn't see and appreciate the full picture until the end. At that point, I could see the mom that others saw: sociable, smart, funny, and strong.

Working on these parent relationships and dissolving old patterns will create more closeness there, and it will also affect how you are with your children. You are their blueprint for relationships. Since your parent relationships are the blueprints, changes here can have a powerful effect on every other relationship in your life, including the one with your Divine.

Let's start with an exercise to loosen up your viewpoint of your parents. I looked at my mom through the standpoint of a teen. As I stepped into other people's viewpoints, I was able to release my biased views. You can start with the parent relationship that may have had more challenging aspects to it. If neither of your parent relationships challenges you, pick someone else and enjoy the process. Notice whatever insights you receive from this exercise.

Viewpoint Exercise

Relax. Slow down the breathing.

Connect in your heart with your Divine.

Ask for support with seeing your parents more clearly.

Bring to mind the parent you are working with. Meet their eyes.

Feel the connection. Breathe.

What aspect of this relationship or what quality do you find challenging?

Bring to mind a situation where you experienced that challenging aspect.

How old are you and what was happening?

See without judgment and without trying to change anything. Simply see it.

Take a deep breath and let that go.

Look at your parent through the eyes of your partner.

Notice what qualities your parent holds in their eyes.

Trust any impression you get without judgment.

See and feel those qualities in your parent.

Take a deep breath and let that go

Look at your parent through the eyes of one of their friends.

Notice what qualities your parent holds in their eyes.

Trust any impression you get without judgment.

See and feel those qualities in your parent.

Take a deep breath and let that go.

Look at your parent through the eyes of your other parent.

Notice what qualities your parent holds in their eyes.

Trust any impression you get without judgment.

See and feel those qualities in your parent.

Take a deep breath and let that go.

Look at your parent through the eyes of your children.

Notice what qualities your parent holds in their eyes.

Trust any impression you get without judgment.

See and feel those qualities in your parent.

Take a deep breath and let that go.

Pretend you are the doorknob. Observe your parent. What do you see?

Breathe. Let it all go.

Open your eyes and journal the various qualities that arose for you from those different viewpoints. Note any surprises that occurred.

Looking through the Lens

We always look through different lenses or filters. We rarely see anyone from an open space of complete clarity. You might experience your partner through positive filters, but they are still in the way of seeing clearly. When you hold onto the positive filter, you are more quickly frustrated when they don't live up to that. I experience this with my husband periodically. Frank is such a wonderfully encouraging person. I view him that way, and when I'm particularly upset and that encouraging personality is not there, I get angry. Where is the Frank I was expecting right now? At least the anger doesn't last because I see what is happening.

I struggled around the time of my mom's funeral with feeling alone in my grief. The encouraging Frank was completely absent and I felt anger on top of the grief. Where is that encouraging personality? Why isn't he being more attentive? Normally, I would see what was really going on and the anger would dissipate, but I was in too deep. I blew up at him. It wasn't his fault that he didn't show up the way I expected. He was dealing with his own issues around all that was happening. Because of what I was experiencing, I didn't allow him that space.

We often look at our children through positive filters, too. When they behave differently than our image of them, instead of being curious about what is going on, we tend to try to suppress their behavior by rebuking them. If we came from a place of curiosity, we may see what is actually happening and have more compassion. Looking at the lens through which we see any situation is so important. People are changing all the time and they will continue to surprise us with their responses. We need to allow others that freedom and extend that to ourselves.

If you'd like to take the Viewpoint Exercise to the next level, go ask five different people what they honestly think of you. Make sure it's an honest invitation on your part. Include your spouse, parents, and children. Write down the answers immediately, word for word. Your mind will quickly change a word here or there to make it less impactful. If you want the truth, write it down before the mind can wiggle out from under the stress. Look at the responses, breathe, and remember that you are all of these things and none of them. Then playfully try on the different viewpoints and see where in your life they may be true. We have many facets and personalities that arise and fall away in different situations. If you can embrace them as I did with my inner critic, magic happens in your relationships.

Charges

You have challenging aspects that get in the way of creating mutually nurturing relationships. We can work on these aspects to allow more freedom in your interactions with others. A healed relationship is one where you allow the other to be who they are and are not thrown off center no matter what they are in. This is a tall order and it's a constant process. The payoff is that you will be able to accept all aspects of your children and allow them to more fully be themselves. You can rekindle the passion that has gone out of your partnership.

We will start with the parents and you'll see it cascade through the rest of the family. Many people have started this process by saying they have a good relationship with their parents. Upon closer inspection they see that they are simply tolerating them, or that they understand why their parents behave a certain way, or they may not express their love toward them. This is because the mind creates stories to cover up the hurtful feelings underneath. It's trying to live up to an image of being a good daughter or son. It's like trying to put a rug over a dirty floor – eventually, the dirt shows. Then, they lash out at their parents or ignore them. We look for these unresolved hurts or places where the feelings have been suppressed. Once released, a more loving and fulfilling relationship arises.

The mind is so quick to run from pain and toward pleasure that, in painful moments, it actually stops the experience and diverts our attention elsewhere (Netflix, ice cream, et cetera.). This diversion often happens without our realizing it. Because the mind stopped us from experiencing the situation all the way through – feeling that humiliation or anger – those feelings are stored in our cells for later. We don't get to skip the experience. We only delay it. That experience sitting in our feeling body is called a "charge" because it's not passive. It's actively sending out signals in order to complete the experience. The signal it sends out causes that personality to arise in someone else so you can try again to complete it. This is why someone can get out of a cab and say, "Don't get in there! He is mean." But you can get in and the driver is friendly. The previous passenger may have been sitting in a charge that activated the driver's mean personality. To neutralize the charge, the passenger needed to experience that situation fully or to see the whole picture. We will talk about seeing the bigger picture later. For now, learn to lean into the feeling and allow it. Stop the pattern.

If a charge is not experienced after multiple times, it becomes a pattern. Later, patterns like these can develop into a personality with a whole set of attributes. The pattern and the personality are using you. You might feel like a victim, wondering why these unfortunate experiences keep repeating in your life. You are not, in fact, a victim. You are the creator. Moreover, since you create these experiences, you can also discreate them. You have to be willing to walk through the fear, allow the anger inside, and feel the sadness.

The good news is that these charges are a great indicator of where to start your healing journey. The other person is playing their part to show you where you have more work to do. This doesn't mean that you allow another to physically abuse you. In fact, a conscious person will run from that situation faster than one who has not worked on their charges. If that happens, you can remove yourself from the situation and then do your internal work.

It takes determination and a strong intention to do this work, but the payoff is huge. You'll receive happiness and freedom. Use this process as often as possible to work on hurts that are stored in your unconscious. Eventually, you'll be able to fully experience them in the moment and not need to revisit them later.

Process for Releasing the Energy behind the Charge

This is simple, but it requires attention and focus.

Close your eyes. Take three deep slow breaths.

Connect in your heart with your Divine.

Ask for support in releasing charges.

Find an interaction from today that hurt you.

It doesn't matter how small the incident.

Place yourself in the situation as if it is happening now.

As it unfolds, let go of the stories in the mind and place all of your attention on whatever feeling arises.

You will likely feel this somewhere in the body.

Place your focus there and stay present with it.

Keep opening into the feeling without making it bigger or holding onto it.

Breathe.

Keep releasing any stories your mind is producing.

Keep focusing your attention.

You may receive an old memory or a belief.

See that memory or belief and keep feeling.

You'll know when the energy behind it starts to release.

Stay with it until it is complete.

Give gratitude to the Divine for the support.

This is a great way to end each day. Look for any pain you've received from interactions with others and release the charges.

Parents

Now we are ready to work on the parent relationship. As a young child, many of your experiences with them may have felt overwhelming at the time. As a result, the mind cut off the experiences and stored them in your system. Now that you are older and more capable of holding this energy, you can fully feel the experiences. As you go through the process, reassure your inner child that he or she is safe. Your adult self can handle this and create a safe space for the child.

If people other than your mother and father raised you, you can work with those guardians. Or you can work with whoever's image comes to you when you close your eyes and begin the process. Then repeat this process at some point with your biological parents, even if you don't remember them.

Start by writing down your intention for this process of healing the parent relationship. Make it in present time or it will always be in your future and not your current experience. It could be something like, "My relationship with my parents is loving and fulfilling." Choose the intention that works for you and write it down.

Parent Relationship Process

This process should be done someplace where you won't be disturbed. You can even do it in the evening before you drop off to sleep. Please stay awake through the whole process.

Close your eyes and take three deep, slow breaths.

Move into your heart area and consciously connect with your Divine.

Your Divine actually runs the process, so your job is to be open to whatever arises.

Start with gratitude to the Divine for specific ways it has helped you.

This creates a deeper bond.

Ask for support with healing the parent relationships so you can experience the intention you wrote above.

Bring your mother before you and look into her eyes for a moment.

Notice how much of your life force energy is moving towards her.

It might be a trickle, a garden hose, or a fire hose.

Just get a sense of it. Breathe and let that go.

Keep looking in her eyes and say whatever your inner child needs to say in simple, direct words. Let her or him freely speak.

As that happens, many different feelings may arise. Allow them all.

Keep bringing your attention to where the highest-intensity feeling lives.

Stay focused on it and let it release.

Keep looking in your mother's eyes and see what else is there.

Maybe you felt unseen or unheard or not good enough.

Keep asking your Divine to show you more, to take you deeper.

Keep breathing.

Keep experiencing.

Take all the time you need.

When you feel complete, look into your mother's eyes.

Notice how much of your life force energy is moving towards her now.

Take three deep, slow breaths and complete the process for now or repeat the above steps with your father.

Be sure to do this with both parents.

Offer gratitude to your Divine for this healing experience.

Notice your interactions with your family over the next week or so. Write down your observations so you can more easily see your progress. Repeat this exercise periodically. Each time it will go deeper into the subconscious.

Many people who have done this work have experienced spontaneous relationship healings. One community member did a similar process in a very sacred space in our center. When she came out of it, she announced that she needed to call her sister. They hadn't talked in eleven years. Her sister was open to connecting and they had a great conversation. The real importance of that moment became clear a year later when their mother moved into her sister's home. If this work hadn't been done, she would have had difficulty visiting her mom.

Another participant reported that, soon after this process was over, she received a call from her father after more than seven years of silence. This inner work has very real outer world impact.

One of the spiritual laws I learned at Oneness University is, "The Outer world is a reflection of the inner world." I've seen variations of this saying in other places too – "as above, so below." Your children can have a very different relationship with you when you have strengthened the ones with your parents.

The more that you practice experiencing the charges, the more you will become aware of them as they are arising. Eventually, you will be able to relax into the charge as it is happening and keep your space clear. This will keep small incidents from escalating into large arguments. This ability to experience the charge as it's happening will significantly enhance your partner relationship.

The inability to deal appropriately with hurts is the main reason many partnerships fail. So many couples start out in love and with great intentions, yet many of them fall apart. Studies suggest that most marriages that fail – about 10 percent, do so in the first one to two years. As the saying goes, "First she talked, and he listened. Then he talked and she listened. Now both talk and the neighbors listen."

Let's look more closely at how this happens.

Anatomy of a Failing Partnership

These hurts seem so insignificant at the time, but they build on each other:

"He ignored me. "

"He didn't take out the trash."

"He worked late and missed our dinner out."

"He doesn't care about me."

The effect of these small complaints is like a grain of sand in an oyster. It hardens. You start to view your partner through a certain lens:

"He is selfish and doesn't care about me."

Now that this lens or viewpoint has formed, the mind will find evidence to support it. The mind will screen out all the times they let you shower first or took you out to a movie that you liked. You will only see where they ignored you, worked late on purpose, or didn't compliment you.

Naturally, this process of collecting evidence causes the filter to harden. It becomes a mask. You no longer relate to the person who is, in fact, constantly changing. You relate instead to a fixed mask. Communication no longer happens, and neither one truly hears the other.

The hurt escalates and you build a wall against that hurt. You feel separate and no longer care about the other. Once you head down this road of indifference, it's a tough journey back.

You give up, decide to cut your losses, and split. Guess what happens in your next relationship? Your unexperienced charges are still with you and have become stronger. The cycle inevitably and powerfully repeats.

There is also collateral damage that you may not even see. You model this behavior for the kids. They are likely to have similar experiences in their relationships.

You now have the key for experiencing the hurts and avoiding this downhill slide. What do you do if you are already part way down that hill and want to stop?

Creating Connection

How do you reconnect?

I discovered this by accident in our relationship. I didn't have a guidebook. I had some judgment around my partner not doing what he said he would, and I had a long list of evidence. Of course, I didn't see all the times he did follow through. On this particular day, we were arguing about him not doing something. In the midst of it, I took a breath and I experienced a moment of grace. I fast forwarded to the end of this conversation and envisioned myself sitting alone because he had stomped off in anger. I didn't want this to happen again. Instead, I asked Spirit for help. I asked that whatever comes out of my mouth serve the highest good. I repeated that request like a mantra.

I looked at Frank who was bright red, waiting to launch his next missile as soon as I gave my retort. What happened next surprised me and almost brought me to my knees. I looked at him in the eyes and said, "I just want to be loved." Some small part of me said, "That's it?"

Before my eyes, all the air went out of Frank like a deflating balloon. He looked at me and said, "I just want to be loved, too."

End of argument.

That was such a profound moment for both of us and we reconnected at a deep level.

Later, I received various similar steps from Oneness and other traditions, but the power of this moment was huge. Many times since then, I have been in arguments where I felt very positional. One had to do with the children's college education. I felt very righteous and looked at him squarely in the eyes. I didn't say anything became I knew that wouldn't get us anywhere. I just stood there, furious with my arms folded across my chest and maintained eye contact. He didn't say anything either and simply held my gaze. After a few minutes, I couldn't hold it anymore. Despite my attempts to hang onto it, the anger dissipated, and I laughed.

The funny thing is that I used to think I could win these arguments. It was clear to me in the first example that winning was impossible. No one was listening to the other's point of view. They were simply preparing their defense. In the second example, knowing this, I didn't try to speak. In charged situations, it's useless to even try getting your point across. There is no winning, only a movement towards more disconnection.

Here are the steps that have worked for me and others. They can transform your experience of your partner or anyone else, especially in the moment where the incident arises.

Stop! Breathe. (Time out.)

Recognize at the core that we all have the same need – to love and be loved.

Slow down your breathing and ask your Divine for help.

Keep eye contact with the other, to show respect and keep the connection alive.

Respond from a place of wanting what is in the highest good here.

Let the words flow out if there are any. Sometimes silence is appropriate.

Becoming

There is another piece to be aware of in the partner relationship. This is the mind's constant habit of becoming. It always wants to work for something in the future rather than being present. When you are dating, you are becoming a couple. When you get married, there is nothing further to become. The mind will then start destroying what it created if it can't become something. One way to work with the mind and avoid that issue is to create a joint project for the two of you that contributes back to society. Working toward a bigger vision of this partnership supports the mind's becoming tendencies and supports your relationship by growing in beautiful ways.

Looking in the Mirror

Partnerships are such powerful relationships because they reflect back to us what we avoid experiencing. That is why this particular relationship can bring maximum pain or maximum pleasure. It can shift from one to the other in an instant unless you raise your awareness.

A powerful practice is to look in that mirror your partner holds and work on your charges. Then, you can respond to them in a loving and appropriate way. This powerful process creates healthier relationships.

You can do this before bedtime while you are lying down.

First, write an intention for how you would like your partnership to be. For example, "My relationship with my partner is open, loving, light, and inspiring."

Partner Process

Start by slowing down your breathing. Take three deep, slow breaths.

Move into your heart area and consciously connect with your Divine.

Remember that your Divine runs the process, and your job is simply to be open to whatever arises.

Start with gratitude to the Divine for specific ways it has helped you.

This creates a deeper bond.

Ask for support with healing of the partner relationship so you can experience the intention you wrote above.

Bring an image of your partner before you and look into their eyes.

Notice how much of your life force energy is moving towards them.

It might be a trickle, garden hose, or fire hose.

Just get a sense of it. Breathe and let that go.

Keep looking in your partner's eyes.

If any charges or strong feelings are arising, be with those until they release.

When complete, move to the next step.

What aspect in your partner challenges you or what do you complain about the most?

It's challenging for you because you carry that quality too and haven't owned it in yourself.

Let go of any resistance that is arising in you.

Ask the Divine to show you where you embody that quality, where you have treated others the way you blame your spouse.

It might show up a little differently.

He might dominate you with words or physically and maybe you do it in an email.

Relax as much as possible and let yourself be shown.

Most of your pain comes from hiding from this.

Freedom comes through seeing.

Once you see where you have treated another in this way, put yourself in the other's shoes.

Feel the pain you caused that other person with that behavior.

Breathe and release.

Look at your partner's eyes again.

Can you accept them for who they are without trying to change them?

Breathe.

Now step into your partner's shoes.

Can you feel what your partner is feeling?

Use your awareness and invite yourself to feel the tensions in your body that they feel in theirs.

Feel their feelings.

Feel where they lack feeling.

Feel the rigidness of their beliefs, the limits of their trust.

Feel their successes and their failures.

Feel their hopes and their dreams.

Fully open to all that this one is experiencing.

See that they are doing the best they can.

Breathe.

Come back to yourself and meet their eyes.

Notice how much of your life force energy is moving towards them.

Breathe and drop into your heart.

Offer gratitude to them for being on this journey with you.

Bless them for all that you want them to have.

Now tune in to receive their blessing.

Open your heart.

Thank them.

Open your eyes.

Write your experience in your journal.

You have seen how unresolved hurts in your primary relationships can create more conflict within your family and community. In order for the intention to spiritually support your family to manifest, you need to start with your own healing. You've begun that process, working through charges and taking steps to heal both your parent and partner relationships. Are you feeling more lightness and freedom inside?

Now, let's dive a little deeper into those places where you have worked on the charges and are still finding it hard to let go of resentment.

Chapter 8

OWNING OUR SHADOW

"Letting go of the need to control is surrender.
Letting go of the hurt is forgiveness.
Letting go of resistance is acceptance.
Letting go of possession is love.
To let go again requires Grace."

~ Sri Amma Bhagavan ~

To be that strong support for your family or your community, you'll need the courage to face the truth, take more responsibility for your life, and be more forgiving. Sometimes, even with the best of intentions, people have trouble forgiving. Despite releasing charges, the resentment is still there. We'll take a closer look at these troubling relationships and how they reflect the parts of yourself you have disowned.

If you can't accept any part of yourself, you can't fully accept your partner or children, and they may not learn to love themselves. If you hold onto resentment toward others, you can't love yourself. Everything is interconnected. It's impossible to isolate the impact of one bad relationship because it will affect everything else. We must develop the courage to face the truth, integrate our shadow parts, and continue to take more responsibility for our lives. Then we need to forgive ourselves and find compassion for our humanness.

Lack of Forgiveness

You have some tools now to support you in healing the hurts, and yet there are some grievances that may continue to run deep in your consciousness. You may feel that you have forgiven over and over. You try to let go again and again, and we are sincere. What happens?

Consciously, you are sincere. Yet your unconscious mind is two billion times stronger than your conscious mind. Everything is stored there, including sabotaging patterns and experiences, As a friend described it, using the conscious mind to overcome the unconscious mind is like shooting a squirt gun into a tidal wave. You are helpless in the face of it. What can you do?

Einstein said that you can't solve a problem from the level of consciousness from which it is created. You'll need to move into a higher state of consciousness where you feel more expanded and connected. From this place, you will receive the grace to let go again.

For the Divine to come to your aid, you need to be aware of the truth of the matter. You must first see how you lack forgiveness. You can't be helped if you are not open to seeing the truth. The mind is tricky here – it will tell you, "You've done a lot of work in this area – give yourself some credit. You have forgiven, but you need help to do better." In this way, the mind is trying to soften the blow, to keep you from seeing the whole truth. You may have tried but you have not forgiven. If you had succeeded, you would have forgotten about the incident and lists of resentments. You have to see the truth, and that is that you lack forgiveness.

What is lack of forgiveness? It's being tied to the past, reliving the same complaint over and over. This repetition creates a groove in consciousness that brings you more of the same. As you give into that viewpoint and nurse this hurt, it becomes a grievance, which can breed hatred. While it may start in only one relationship, it won't stay there. If allowed to grow, it eventually creeps into all of your relationships like a cancer. This leads to self-hatred. If you can't forgive others, you can't forgive yourself. Let's take a closer look at why nothing in this realm can exist in isolation.

Interconnection

Everything is interconnected. If you truly look at the shirt you are wearing, you will realize that the whole world was involved in bringing it to you. Farmers grew the cotton using water, earth, and sunshine. Cotton pickers used machines to gather it. Factories turned the cotton into a shirt, which was designed by another group of people. Trucks delivered it to warehouses, which sent them out in trucks to the store from which you purchased it. Your shirt represents a worldwide network of resources. Take that in and look at your shirt. With this perspective you might feel gratitude for the gift of this clothing.

Everyone is now familiar with the concept of interconnection due to the internet, which allows people from all over the world to collaborate on projects and communicate easily and instantly.

The internet is simply an outer manifestation of what exists inside each of us. We have an internal network that connects us to all manner of resources. Ancient and indigenous cultures are aware of this and use this internal internet for navigating their lives. Our western culture has used science and technology to create the external version.

Let's take a closer look at this web of light that physically connects all of us, through a visualization.

Interconnectedness Contemplation

Close your eyes.

Take three slow, deep breaths.

Connect in your heart with your Divine.

Feel that presence enveloping you.

Ask for an experience of the interconnectedness of all life.

Breathe.

Accept whatever images or feelings arise for you and be with that for a few minutes.

Look a little more closely at this web of interconnection.

It may appear as bright strands of light connecting everyone.

It's flexible and bright.

Whatever anyone is feeling flows through those channels into the whole network.

Take a few moments to observe.

Now notice the connection between you and your loved ones.

See the quality of the light that connects you.

Now, see the connection between you and someone you haven't fully forgiven.

You might see a thick, rigid cord connecting both of you, creating constriction.

One tugs and the other feels it. You may feel trapped.

Breathe.

Tune into the hurt that is present. Feel whatever is arising.

As soon as the energy releases, you might see that cord become light and flexible again.

Breathe.

Widen back again and see the whole network.

Anchor in this sense of interconnectedness.

Offer gratitude to your Divine for this experience.

When you are ready, open your eyes.

What did you notice about this experience? Were you able to see and feel your connectedness with all beings? As you relax into this viewpoint, you'll start to feel the connection that is always there, even with strangers that you meet. You'll be more aware of your impact on others and your environment. As you continue to tune in, you'll experience a deeper interconnectedness with nature.

Now we'll look at the nature of resentments – how they grow and become lodged in your system.

Forming Resentments

Anything that is born on this earth plane wants to grow. We exist in a cycle of creation, growth, and destruction. Once something or someone is born, they are either in a state of growing or dying. There is no steady state. The cells in your body constantly regenerate. The plants in your yard grow as long as you water and feed them. They will continue to grow out of control unless you prune them. Then, they continue to grow in a more compact space.

It's the same with ideas. Any idea born on this plane of existence wants to grow. As it grows, it consumes energy. The more thoughts associated with the idea, the more energy it consumes.

It's using more and more of your energy and you may not even be aware of it.

Thoughts are energy particles with mass and weight. You can actually see them floating in the air around you. That's why people often have the same thoughts at the same time. You've experienced this with your friends where both of you say the same thing at once. It's also a well-known phenomenon that many inventions in history were discovered by more than one person at the same time in different parts of the world. These are called multiple discoveries and include inventions such as the crossbow, blast furnace, and magnets. These inventors were pursuing similar areas of interest and tuned into the same thoughts.

Where we place our attention also has a measurable effect. Our attention directs energy. Look at the phenomenon of gaper's blocks that form on the highways after an accident. As more people slow down to look, more people are drawn to look at it. The more people viewing it, the more attracting energy it contains, and others feel the pull to look at the accident. It's hard to resist that pull.

Any idea that is born wants to grow, and this collection of thoughts has energy. As it grows, more and more of our energy and attention attracts and focuses on it. This causes us to naturally become more interested in it. As we focus more and more, it gathers more thoughts and consumes more of our energy. We can't easily turn our attention away from it. We walk around watching a movie in our head or in a virtual reality of our own making.

Resentments are a collection of thoughts with a lot of energy behind them. Usually, they have been operating in our unconscious for a period of time. These grievances continually feed on our energy to stay alive. As long as we continue to carry them, we feel drained and tired. If they continue to grow unchecked, we reach a point where we can't take in any more input. We might withdraw into our room away from people. Even looking around the room might trigger more thoughts, so we turn out the lights. Now, alone in a dark room, we continue to suppress our painful thoughts and start spiraling down into depression. The life force energy has gone out.

Perhaps you can find the motivation within yourself to do something about these resentments, even if it's just to reclaim your life force energy.

The Road Back

What can you do? First, become aware of the truth. You need to bring the focus of your attention to what is happening inside of you. Here is an example that one of our community members, Donna, shared.

She was enjoying herself at a birthday party until someone she didn't even know looked at her in a funny way. Because Donna felt awkward in social situations, she experienced a wave of shame washing over her. Donna remembered to allow the experience. She stayed with the shame, without resistance. Within a few minutes, Donna saw a memory of herself as a four-year-old in a playground, covered with dirt. Other kids laughed at her because she was so messy. As she kept her attention on how the four-year-old felt, she saw that child take on a belief. "I am funny-looking, and no one wants to play with me." That idea, born in that moment, continued to grow for a lifetime. Because she finally saw the truth, it was over. The next time someone looked at her in that way, she only felt curiosity. The shame was gone.

Seemingly inconsequential moments, such as someone making a face at us, can allow for healing. Like a big ball of yarn, pull on the string and it goes back to childhood.

Use this process to follow your issue back to the source.

Process to Find the Source of Resentment

Close eyes. Breathe. Connect.

Bring to mind a situation that still triggers you.

Feel the hurt.

Let go of resistance.

Be with the feeling.

Keep your attention there.

Let go of any stories that are arising.

Keep breathing and keep feeling.

Follow this feeling by moving in the direction of the most pain.

It may lead you back through other life situations.

Keep feeling.

Stay with it.

Go all the way back. How old are you?

What's happening?

Can you see the belief you took on?

What are you saying to yourself?

Breathe.

See it and release the energy on the breath.

Breathe in self-forgiveness.

Release anything left from this experience on the outbreath.

Offer gratitude to the Divine for this experience.

Write any insights in your journal. You might begin to see more places where this belief or this experience has impacted your life. Practice this one as many times as it takes to get comfortable with the process and to see the truth. As Sri Bhagavan says, "to see is to be free."

The Nature of Resentments

I grew up in a family of bright and articulate people. Both my brother and sister grew up to be lawyers and successful litigators, so winning arguments against them was hopeless. I had to develop different strategies, such as becoming invisible. I stockpiled my resentments because I didn't have a safe way to speak out or to release them. Since I wasn't quick enough argue my points, I had to have my ammunition – my list of resentments ready to fire when an opportunity arose.

Long after I divorced my first husband, I carried around a list of resentments ready to fire at him when appropriate. I thought that it was a relatively harmless practice. Then, in a contemplation, after experiencing the interconnectedness of all life, I had a vision of those resentments that I thought were in cold storage, burning me like hot coals until I dropped them. The simple act of holding onto them was hurting me, not my ex-husband. That realization gave me motivation to release the list of grievances that I had been carrying for decades. Seeing at this level is transforming.

An extraordinary thing happened once I did this. I picked up the phone. This was not a voluntary act. I called him and thanked him profusely for all that he had done for the kids, and I meant it. Once I let go, I could appreciate for the first time all the hard work that he put into his relationship with them and with my mom, and I was deeply grateful. I knew I had successfully let go of some big stories that were keeping me stuck. I have seen the light go on for many others who have also released their resentments. Many of them didn't even realize they were carrying them.

This is another approach to working with difficult issues. I find it especially useful for seeing how these resentments infiltrate every area of our lives. It may provide more incentive for you to work on them.

Resentment Process

Take out your journal and draw yourself in the middle of the paper. Put your issue there. For me, it was an issue with my partner where he dropped the ball and it landed on my plate. Now, start drawing on the paper all the places in your life where this shows up: at home, work, with friends, current timeframe, in your earlier years, et cetera. Write as many instances as you can using words, stick figures, or other images. Take up as much of the paper as you can.

Connect inside for a moment. Slow down your breathing.

Ask to be shown other instances where this issue is showing up in your life.

Draw those on the paper.

Keep tuning in and drawing more instances until that feels complete.

Breathe and take a look at everything you have drawn.

Then close your eyes.

Breathe.

Connect with your Divine and ask: "What is the underlying belief?

(In my case it was, "It's all up to me.")

Accept whatever you get, even if it appears unrelated.

Write it down.

Now let's take this process a step further.

Look at your paper.

Close your eyes.

Connect in your heart with your Divine
Bring the issue to mind.
See all the other situations where this issue has arisen.
Ask to be shown where else this shows up.
Step back and see the whole landscape:
All the places, people, and situations that are related to this issue.
Recognize that you are feeding it energy, keeping all of these situations alive.
What is the payoff you are receiving from keeping it alive?
Accept any answer without judgment.
What is it you are really wanting (freedom, love, …)_____?
In the name of (freedom, love…) _____, I choose to release it.
See it disappear.
Consciously connect with the Divine.
Experience the (freedom, love…) _____
From this place, look at the situation again and see if there is any residual stickiness or resistance, then ask your Divine to help you let it go.
Breathe and relax even more deeply into the Presence.
This is the space where anything is possible.
In this space, create a new intention for this situation or relationship.
Offer gratitude.
Keep that connection to the Divine alive as you open your eyes.
Write down your new intention.

"To let go of the hurt is forgiveness."
~ Sri Amma Bhagavan ~

Owning Our Shadow

Let's take this a little deeper. The issue that shows up as a resentment may be pointing to a behavior that you don't want to own in yourself. Resenting my partner for dropping the ball is an easy way for me not to look at where I do that. While we can release the resentment through the above process, it will reappear if we don't handle the underlying resistance to owning this behavior within ourselves.

Many of the things you might find unforgiveable are behaviors that you have been taught are "bad:" betrayal, meanness, hatred, and jealousy, to name a few. Since the mind is based in duality, these naturally exist alongside their opposites. Everyone experiences them. I have experienced loving my partner one minute, hating him the next, and then loving him again. This is the conditional love that comprises most of our experience. Only in a high state of consciousness can we experience the unconditional love that has no opposite. This is another reason why your connection with the Divine is so critical. That's where qualities such as love, peace, and joy exist without an opposite.

We've experienced all of these behaviors, but because we label them as bad, we self-righteously point them out in others. It's too painful to look inside at the places we have been inexcusably harsh or selfish. If we can't take ownership of all of these behaviors, then we can't fully accept our children, partner, or friends as they are. Ultimately, to be that loving spiritual leader, we must be able to be present without judgment.

Generally, people shift in their seats at this point until I explain the difference between accepting and condoning these behaviors. If you can't accept your child being mean at times, then you will be highly charged when you see that behavior. Any interaction you have from that charged place will escalate conflict and go in the opposite direction of what you desire. If you can instead be fully present to the meanness, you might inquire what is happening with them. Perhaps they have an injury, or another child just yelled at them. It's your aversion to the behavior that causes problems, not necessarily the behavior itself. In order to accept these behaviors in your children, you'll need to start by accepting them in yourself.

One of our community members is triggered by seeing others receive special treatment. She becomes confrontational, pulling everyone's attention back to herself. It's hard on everyone, especially her. She worked through this issue in our group and is now able to see it as it arises. Instead of being victim to it and lashing out, she realizes, "Oh, that's me wanting to feel special." Her realization is a huge gift to everyone.

Let's look through the grocery list for our favorite behaviors (meanness, sloppiness, stupidity, selfishness). Jealousy is one that I tend to push aside when it catches me off guard. Let's take ownership of jealousy in this exercise.

Embodying Resisted Behaviors Process

This is a great exercise to do with a coach, but you can play with it on your own. First connect with your inner child that is curious, playful and open to learning.

Tune into the behavior – jealousy.

Exist for a moment as jealousy.

Let go of any resistance and fully embody that energy.

Let it speak through you in the first person.

Listen to what jealousy has to say.

If you have a coach, they can write down the messages.

If not, you can record it and take notes later.

When I did this exercise, the message was: "I am here to get you moving. You've been talking about writing a book for a long time. It's time to take action." Jealousy had arisen for me when three different friends said they were writing books. In this case, it served a useful purpose. Perhaps you'll see that the energy you are working with – jealousy, meanness or selfishness, moved you into action, protected you or gave you an insight.

The next step is to transmute the energy.

You may have an intellectual understanding from this exercise that jealousy or the behavior you have resisted serves a purpose. See if you can fully embrace and own it. If you can learn to love it all, then you can whole-heartedly love and guide your family.

Process to Transmute Energy

Close your eyes.

See this behavior or jealousy that you have resisted in its wholeness.

See its useful purpose in this situation.

See how it can also be destructive.

Feel the energy of jealousy.

Breathe it into your heart.

Open your heart as much as possible.

Allow the heart to transmute this energy into love.

Breathe in the jealousy and breathe out liberation or freedom three times slowly.

Breathe and let go.

Connect with your Divine and breathe in self-forgiveness.

Let your heart fill with the love that is present.

Self-Forgiveness

Self-forgiveness is a critical practice on this path. Whenever you face a situation of needing to forgive another, you need to extend that same forgiveness to yourself because some part of you feels guilty about not forgiving or about allowing the situation to happen. Forgiveness of the other and the self go hand-in-hand. You can connect in the heart with the Divine, feel the guilt or shame that is present and allow the charge to release. Then open to the love and compassion that is always present when you are connected.

Compassion arises from the recognition that we are all very much alike. You've seen how the "unforgiveable" behaviors you blame others for are ones that you also carry. If you can remember how alike we are in those moments, you can respond from a more compassionate place. When you embrace all of those behaviors in others and yourself as part of our humanness then self-forgiveness naturally flows and you start loving yourself more fully.

You've seen how the mind creates images of what it wants to be – kind and loving – and it judges your behavior accordingly. Similarly, it creates judgments about the people in our lives and collects evidence to reinforce its beliefs. When you buy into these stories, it creates more conflict and pain. You've seen that when you project blame on another, it's because you haven't owned that behavior in yourself. To acknowledge and own the "unacceptable" qualities helps you see the ways you are like the other. The mind tries to find the ways you are different. You've seen how interconnected we are and that any work that we do has a ripple effect. You've seen how grievances feed off of your energy. You are beginning to take self-responsibility for your life. This is a great lesson for your children to learn.

Chapter 9

SEE THE BIG PICTURE

Thoughts, wrapped up with emotions, attract your attention and drain your energy. To solidify that thoughts are not important, I'll show you how to simply observe them from a place of silence to see the bigger picture. Your attention is naturally pulled to the charged thoughts, so it's a practice of seeing that and letting go. As you rest more and more in this place of watching, you'll feel a deep inner peace. Then, you can handle unexpected issues with family, coworkers, and larger community without being thrown off-center. You will have access to your intelligence.

"The content of the mind is not important. Experiencing it is."
~ *Sri Amma Bhagavan* ~

This idea disturbed me at first because I thought there might be a brilliant thought in my mind that I would miss if I let it go. I kept searching my mind until I finally realized most of my thoughts were negative. Intrigued, I carefully observed and wrote down as many thoughts as I could. There were a few neutral ones commenting on what I saw or reminded me of what was next on my schedule, but most of my thoughts were negative – bringing up fears and old, hurtful stories. The brilliant thoughts came spontaneously when I was completely relaxed and absorbed in my work or in the shower. These thoughts were of a different quality and from a source other that the mind.

The mind is essentially a measurement tool, taking the past and projecting it into the future. It measures what is happening now against past experience to see if there is a threat facing you in the moment. It tries to protect you from harm. You don't need to banish the mind – just don't focus on it. You need the mind to navigate the external world. The trouble arises when you apply your analytical skills to the internal world. The analysis is the issue. It gets completely tied up with questions such as, "Why do I exist?" or, "Why is this happening to me?"

There is no answer to these questions. I tripped over this one many times before. I notice that the question, "Why?" puts me into victim mode and keeps me from moving forward in my life. I spiral down into the projection, into a lower level of consciousness, instead of expanding out of it. When I catch this downward spiral, I set an intention around what I prefer to experience.

While the content isn't important, experiencing is. You've been practicing this by facing the charges from your relationships and experiencing them. An emotion wrapped with a story is a powerful attention grabber. In that practice, one of the steps is to let go of the story or let go of the content of the mind, which is keeping you stuck in it. This type of circular thinking – worrying about an issue – is like being stuck in a whirlpool. Life is passing you by and you are going around and around this issue. By experiencing the charge and dropping the story, you separate the emotion from the content so you can move back into flow.

It's easy to tell if you are being pulled into that mind trap because the feeling of the situation gets denser and you feel contracted. Remember that any interactions or any decisions made from that disconnected state will produce conflict. Being aware of what state we are in, whether contracting or expanding, is important.

Being Present

Now you can move toward that desirable state of experiencing peace. People talk about world peace and even demonstrate for peace. Since our outer world is reflecting our inner world, let's see if we can find peace there. How would it be to feel peace regardless of your outer circumstances? It's possible. From that place, you can make clear decisions.

In this fast-paced world, it seems our peace is more profoundly disturbed. I used to have this fantasy that if I could go lay on the beach for a few days, everything would be fine. I was looking for the world to stop so I could have some downtime. Unfortunately, my mind was at the beach with me, constantly disturbing my peace. I've tried other approaches, like rollercoaster riding and skydiving. Those moments of speeding downhill or dropping through the air were such addictive highs. The high came from being fully present, experiencing the moment. My mind was blank. I went as often as I could, not realizing why these activities drew me in. Oddly enough, when I started on my personal journey beginning with Shematrix Mystery School, my desire to ride rollercoasters completely dropped away.

The thrill of flying through the air was an experience of being alive and in the present moment. I didn't have that anywhere else. My mind was silent, and I simply experienced the moment fully, but the feeling didn't last. My mind would be highly agitated with fear right up until the moment of the drop, and then it went quiet. As soon as the ride was over, my mind was back. When I worked on my internal world and faced my fears with the help of the women's collective, I experienced that place of being fully alive and fulfilled. I could be in that space for longer periods of time. I didn't have to go looking for bigger and bigger roller coasters or stand in line for an hour to get a few moments of it.

Earth Changes

Right now, we are not only experiencing a fast-paced society, but also an increasing rate of change. Even the Earth's frequency, the Schuman resonance, is speeding up. Our minds are unable to cope, and they easily get overwhelmed. I used to think the Earth was headed in the wrong direction. Meditation is about slowing down the brain waves, and here, society and even Mother Earth is pushing us in the opposite direction. I found a fascinating explanation on Dr. Joe Dispenza's log, "What does the Schumann Resonance mean?" He talks about various brain waves. At the root of all our thoughts and emotions is the communication between the neurons in our brains. Electrical impulses from masses of neurons communicating produce brain waves that can be measured by placing sensors on the scalp. Our brain waves change according to what we are doing and feeling. The slower waves, such as Alphas, are dominant in meditative states, whereas the faster Beta waves dominate our normal waking hours. At even higher frequencies, Gamma waves, initially dismissed as noise, were discovered to be highly active in an expanded state of consciousness, such as unconditional love.

Joe explains in his article that the brain waves of an enlightened being are Gamma waves. While the Beta brain waves are usually associated with a brain that is stressed, over-aroused and imbalanced, we have to move through these stressful Beta waves to reach the much higher frequency Gamma rays where we are in a super conscious state experiencing true love and compassion. Everything is conspiring to move us into higher states of consciousness. The increasing rate of change is helping us to do that. Rather than being carried away by it or looking to escape it, let's stand in it and find that inner stillness. You will need to practice meditation to keep grounded and centered.

Meditation

This requires effort. Many times, people come to the FHC saying they have never been able to meditate by themselves and are surprised when it is so easy here. Being with a racing mind makes it hard to sit still. We need to raise our consciousness. This is easier to do in a sacred space and in a group setting. We'll talk about how to do it on your own in the next chapter. Beginners put their effort into stopping the mind, which isn't possible. We start with the breath, which is linked to the mind and body. It's often represented as a triangle:

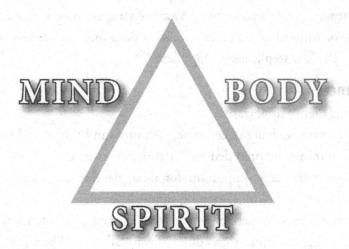

Working on any one part can affect the other two. Since It can be difficult to keep the body still, we work with the breath. Slowing down the breath is the first step in every process in this book because it slows the mind.

Direct your attention to the breath, which can also be thought of as a life-giving force or Spirit. Another word for inhale is "inspire," or to bring in Spirit. Remember the power of focusing your attention and how you used that to release the energy behind the charges. In that process, your attention is like a magnifying glass that is focused on a piece of paper in the sun. What happens? The sun magnifies, heats the paper, and burns it, just like your charges.

You might even feel heat in the body as you place your attention on the charge. Sustained focus of attention transforms. In that process, you may have noticed that your attention wanders and you must keep bringing it back. The more sustained your focus, the more powerfully your attention burns through the charges. Practice is important.

In this chapter, you'll need to practice sustained effort in a different way. You'll become more aware of your awareness. From this place of witnessing, you'll experience a deep inner peace and stillness. The first step is becoming silent.

Silence

Why is silence important?

Herman Melville once wrote, "All profound things and emotions of things are preceded and attended by silence."

Outer silence is important for us to develop the inner stillness. If you are talking, listening to music, or watching television, your mind remains active. As you keep placing your attention on the breath, your mind slows down. Eventually, it will become quieter with fewer thoughts. Once you get more distance from the thoughts, you are less likely to get caught up in them. A sense of inner peace and stillness develops. Imagine a large stadium that is empty except for a small radio playing in one of the seats. Where would you choose to sit if you want peace of mind – next to the radio? That's where we automatically go. Choose instead to sit across the stadium from it. The radio will keep playing. Thoughts will keep flowing. With distance, you'll have peace. You don't need to know the content of the thoughts or what is playing on the radio.

As you keep returning your attention to the breath, you will start to tune into that silence. Many books have been written about the positive benefits of meditation on the body and mind (reducing blood pressure, decreased pain, increased immune function). Many doctors now even suggest meditation to their patients. Raising the awareness around the importance of silence is a newer conversation in our culture, perhaps because our environments have become much louder. We are bombarded with loud music in restaurants and televisions while standing in line at an amusement park or pumping gas. A study reported in *Science Says Silence is Much More Important to Our Brains Than We Think*, by Rebecca Beris, reported that our brains actually require silence to actively organize and evaluate the information it takes in, both internally and externally.

Researchers measured the effects of sound and silence on the brains of mice and were surprised to find that two hours of silence in a day caused the hippocampus to create new cells. Silence quite literally nurtures the brain.

I've heard it said many times that you should meditate at least 20 minutes a day. If you are too busy to do that, then you need to meditate an hour a day. The study above sheds light on why that's true. A busy person likely has more data to integrate. To make intelligent decisions, the brain needs that downtime. This study found it is more effective to meditate in silence than to use relaxing music.

Meditation really does make us more intelligent. If your mind is active, it's helpful to raise your energy before meditating. At our center, we maintain a high-energy field so participants can easily drop in. You can raise your energy through various techniques, including breathing practices, chanting, movement, singing bowls, or connecting powerfully with your Divine. You can experiment and see what works for you.

The Witness

We will now experience the witness state, which is beyond all description and can only be experienced. It's a state of seeing or actually being the big picture. When you are caught up in your thoughts, you make decisions from inside the issue that is grabbing your attention. It's a limited and biased viewpoint. You can't make intelligent choices from that place. It's a case of not being able to see the forest through the trees. When you are hurried and worried about your list of things to get done, your children know you are distracted. That's when they ask for things they want, like ice cream. They know you are more likely to say yes because they can feel you are off-center. The cost of giving into this request may be small. What about the cost of negotiating a contract from a place of fear? Being able to detach from the issue, step back, and see the bigger picture is important. The meditation here will start to train you to widen back. Eventually, you will be the witness.

The witness is the one that is always quietly in the background watching. It doesn't get thrown off-center or distracted. You can say that there is an inherent trust that everything will be all right, but the witness doesn't need that. It just is. It's awareness. We can't explain it. We can only point to it.

As part of this meditation, we will be using alternate nostril breathing to turn our attention inwards and quiet the mind in a more powerful way. This type of breathing is also recommended to reduce stress and anxiety, and to promote overall well-being.

Alternate Nostril Breathing Procedure

Sit in a comfortable position with your back straight and feet on the floor.

Place your left-hand palm up on your left thigh.

Bring the index finger of the left hand to the base of the thumb.

Open your right hand, palm up.

Bring the index and middle finger down onto the palm, keeping your ring and pinkie fingers extended.

Keep both hands in these postures for the duration of the breathing exercise.

Lift the right hand towards the nose.

Exhale completely and then use your right thumb to close your right nostril.

Inhale through your left nostril and then close the left nostril with the fingers of your right hand.

Open the right nostril and exhale through this side.

Inhale through the right nostril and close this nostril.

Open the left nostril and exhale through the left side.

This is one cycle.

Nadi Shodhana Pranayama
or Alternate Nostril Breathing

Witness Meditation

Read through this process so you are clear before you start.

Close your eyes and take three deep slow breaths.

Begin alternate nostril breathing for five minutes to turn the mind inwards.

Now, for five minutes, focus on the flow of breath as it comes in through the nose, to the lungs, and back out again.

Bring your total attention there. Keep releasing thoughts. Follow the flow.

For five minutes, bring your attention to the gap between the inhale and exhale.

Notice how you have shifted from flowing with the breath to watching the breath.

Now, move through that gap between the inhale and exhale into the background.

Your breathing is in the foreground

Widen back.

You are aware of the breathing.

Notice your awareness.

You are aware of thoughts.

If you notice you are thinking, bring your attention back to awareness.

Instead of watching thoughts, become aware of your awareness.

Continue for as long as you can or for at least ten minutes.

Do this practice at least once a day if possible. This will heighten your awareness in everyday life. You will have some distance from your thoughts. You will start to become aware in the moment when you are triggered, and experience it rather than push it away. You will start to notice when you are off-center and not make decisions from that place. You will start to hear your internal guidance more clearly. You will start to experience that inner stillness even in the midst of chaos. So many benefits arise from this meditation. Even if you only experience the witness state for a moment, it will have a huge impact.

Revisiting Intentions

Now that you are able to get some distance from your thoughts and are more aware around experiencing whatever is arising, let's revisit your intentions.

Go back to one of the intentions you set for yourself at the beginning of this book – the one about being that strong spiritual support for your family.

You might notice when you look at it that you have some reservations.

"I'm not ready to be that!" Feel that resistance in your body and whatever else is there. Be present to it.

Watch for thoughts like:

"I don't want that responsibility."

"Why me?"

"Can't my partner help?"

See these thoughts and experience all that is arising from this.

Be present with whatever arises – frustration, fear, anger.

Let go of resistance.

While you experience the feeling, notice if you are drawn deeper into it. If so, widen back into a more expanded viewpoint. You still feel without resistance, but you are not spiraling down with it. You are fully present to all that is happening. In this place, you'll observe various obstacles arise. Bring the focus of your attention to them and watch the energy behind the obstacles release.

Intentions versus Positive Thinking

Intentions are not the same as positive thinking. Often, people use positive thinking to avoid feeling their resistance to what they are trying to create.

You say, "I am that spiritual support for my family."

Your internal voice says, "I am not"

You say, "I am," and it says, "I am not!"

Notice that with positive thinking you are empowering both sides – the negative and the positive side of this intention. In a sense, they cancel each other out and the byproduct is a lot of extra thoughts and noise in your head.

Here, we are looking at the intention and allowing the charges that are in the way to arise. As you release the energy behind them, it creates more space for the intention to grow.

Empowering Intentions

Take three deep, slow breaths.

Connect with the Divine in your heart and ask for support with your intention.

Take a look at the intention and read it to yourself.

Notice where you feel any sensations, resistances, or thoughts about it.

Be present to that experience.

If the thought is, "I'm not ready," be with that thought and feel the emotion tied to it.

Be with it until the charge releases.

Look at your intention again and see if there are any more charges.

If none surface, ask your Divine to help you experience anything in the way of this intention.

When that feels complete, tune in to see if there is an action you need to take right now to support this intention.

Offer gratitude to the Divine for the support.

Take a deep breath and open your eyes.

You are well on the way to becoming a strong support for others since you are able to ride the waves of everyday life and stay centered, calm, and clear.

Let's take it up a notch and invite the Divine to play with us and create miracles.

Chapter 10

EXPECT MIRACLES

I used to say I was "lucky" when I experienced coincidences, such as finding a $10 bill laying alongside the road when I forgot my wallet that day. As I grew in consciousness, I recognized there was a universal intelligence behind everything and I noticed more synchronicities happening, which put me in a state of gratitude. When my relationship with the Divine deepened, I experienced miracles that my mind could not believe were possible. As the miracles multiplied and that relationship flowered, I relied on grace to do the heavy lifting in my life. You can too. We will take a closer look at your relationship with your Divine and how to become interdependent.

"Why, sometimes I've believed as many as six impossible things
before breakfast."

~ ***Lewis Carroll,*** *Alice in Wonderland* ~

Miracles

I love this quote. Whenever I feel like my schedule or my tasks are looming and impossibly demanding, I'm reminded of this quote. The mind often makes the future seem quite bleak, so we need to feed it with possibilities and stories of miracles. What seems possible to us now was impossible only ten years ago. I'm reminded of the old Dick Tracy cartoons where he talked into his watch. I thought that was fantasy, but now it's reality. Whatever can be envisioned can be created. The mind needs to be reminded that what it perceives as a limitation is simply not true.

In 1954, Roger Bannister broke the four-minute record for running a mile. Since that event, over 1,400 athletes have run the mile in under four minutes because they believed it was possible. Miracles, by definition, are things that happen that the mind thought wasn't possible. By acknowledging these miracles and sharing them with others, the mind opens, and miracles start to multiply.

Recently, a friend of mine brought a faith healer to our community to offer sessions. I was excited about meeting him, experiencing his work, and seeing what he could do for the pain in my knees.

Two months earlier, I had agreed to walk the El Camino path through northern Spain in a few months, even though my knees were in chronic pain. I was excited, but then, I found walking even three miles a day to be painfully difficult. Walking 500 miles in 35 days seemed like a huge leap of faith. I told the healer about it, prayed hard, and watched as he reached his hands through my skin and under the kneecap. He pulled out a piece of calcified material that looked like a small pebble. I watched my mind slide all over the place, trying to get a grip as he did it again. Despite the fact that I've heard of this before and believed in it, the actual experience unglued my mind. I gingerly felt these small pebbles he pulled out from under each kneecap as he explained how they were pressing on my nerves and causing pain. I quietly said thank you and climbed down the massage tables onto wobbly knees. There was a slight scar behind each knee that healed within hours. Three days later, when I was allowed to start walking again, there was no pain. I've since walked many seven-mile days without knee pain. I watched the mind try to negate what happened, but the evidence was undeniable. Fortunately, I heard many stories of miracle healings from others, so I had enough faith in the process to receive healing. Faith is required from both the patient and the reverend for him to go inside and find the obstructing tissue to release.

The more you listen to miracles and share miracles, the less the mind will get in the way of what you want to create in your life. Believing six impossible things before breakfast is great advice.

Miracles are a gift from the Divine, and the stronger your relationship, the more they occur. Your personal Divine is happy to give you what you want, but you have to do your part. As a parent, you may understand this. You want to shower your children with all they want, in an effort to make them happy. At that same time, you recognize that some of what they want is not good for them and might cause them trouble later. You have a higher viewpoint and use discernment in deciding what to give them. The same is true in your relationship with the Divine.

Divine Hand

One way to deepen this relationship is to recognize and acknowledge all that our Divine does for us. First, we need to see that the Divine hand is operating in our lives. Then, we can offer gratitude and share with others. Our relationships will deepen tremendously. You can feel in yourself the joy of giving to someone who is truly grateful. You want to give them more. The Divine operates the same way.

I used to think that the Divine hand only operated in my life when something happened that I obviously didn't do. For example, if a parking space opened up by the front door, I could acknowledge it as the Divine hand. If I successfully completed a project at work, that was my hand. I figured out how to get that job done. Now, I see clearly how the Divine hand was there all along – starting with receiving the project, connecting me to the resources I needed, keeping me determined and focused, and helping me finish on time. The mind wanted to take full credit for it, of course. If I bought into that, I would miss out on a powerful business partner – my Divine. Many people I know consciously turn their business decisions over to their Divine, and in return offer 10 or 20 percent of the revenue to charity in gratitude. They've had extraordinary gains. It takes faith, courage, and the ability to listen to the inner guidance without the filters of our old patterns, charges, and hidden agendas. This is easier said than done.

I had to learn the hard way. I thought I was partnering with the Divine, relinquishing full control, but then I saw the sneaky ways my mind took control back. This took the form of contingency plans and exit strategies. I realized that being strong and independent (in control) was a value that ran deep in my family and our culture. We watched a lot of westerns growing up. It wasn't about collaboration. It was about winning.

I was competitive most of my life until I entered the Shematrix Mystery School and had to release that. I was shown time and time again the effects my competitive nature had on the people I worked with. Seeing the pain I caused others eventually toned down that competitive instinct. Competition itself is not the problem. Rather, it's what we do with it. When the mind plays games to make someone else look bad so I can look "good," that destroys relationships. I was grateful for the patience and love of my sisters to move through it. Because I am able to recognize that competitive instinct and move towards collaboration, I now experience a beautiful sense of interdependence with my Divine. I am dependent on the Divine for resources and support. In turn, the Divine is dependent on me to offer resources and support to others. That is one way that our partnership is operating powerfully.

This journey is not for the faint of heart. Living an extraordinary life in partnership with the Divine requires us to let go of so many ideas of where our security and joy is sourced from. In my family, financial security was highly valued, so we were all highly educated. I am grateful for that. I understand the appeal and the benefits of financial security. When I lost that security, I was terrified until I learned to find it inside. The only security in a world that changes so rapidly is with my connection to my Divine and the guidance that comes from there. This story illustrates the point.

An older holy man in Indonesia walked through the woods one day and suddenly got the urge to climb a tree. He had not done this since he was a boy, but he followed his guidance. As he climbed to the upper branches of the tree, he saw the reason for this urge. A tsunami was approaching, and he would have been swept away if he had stayed on the ground. This is the type of security only our Divine guidance can offer. We can more readily appreciate and open to the Divine when we better understand its qualities.

Divine Qualities

We continually search for other humans to give us what only the Divine can give, and then we blame them for falling short of our expectations. Most of us are dealing with childhood wounds because of times when our parents just weren't there for us. Maybe they were away working when we needed them, or maybe they were dealing with their own internal trauma and could not offer us the love we sought.

Since all of us feel the same core need to be loved and give love, this creates a longing inside. The form of love you are used to experiencing is the one that can shift in a moment to anger and then back to love. It's conditional. You might be able to feel love for your child even when they are angry, but it might be more difficult with a teen or spouse. Conditional love always comes with its opposite, hate. Only in a high state of consciousness can you experience unconditional love, yet you continue to seek it from family and friends. If this need is met in your relationship with the Divine, then you can love your family without expecting something back.

The Divine qualities have no opposites. They transcend the duality we experience here. Unconditional love that we seek is only possible with the Divine. It simply is a field of love that exists everywhere. Like sunlight, it doesn't discriminate against who receives it. It's for everyone. All the Divine qualities – joy, wisdom, compassion, peace – have no opposite. You might have had glimpses of these qualities. Even a few seconds of that will change your life. As your relationship deepens, you will experience more of these qualities.

Seven-Step Prayer

Now that you are clear about this Divine relationship and the possibility of miracles in your life, you can ask for help in the form of a powerful seven-step prayer that I learned from Oneness University. You can ask for whatever you want – solutions to your financial, health, and relationship problems. The Divine is happy to respond because the more you feel fulfilled, the more you naturally contribute to the well-being of others.

Connect with the Divine and Be Open to Receiving Help

Step 1 is to ask for help. Since you need to solve your problems from a higher level of consciousness than the one that created them, you need to turn to the Divine. You must come from a place of helplessness in order to receive help. This is such a resisted state in our western society, where we love watching action heroes always overcome adversity. We are programmed to be independent and self-sufficient, and therefore our prayers go unanswered. Helplessness equates to weakness. We may have been told we need to surrender, and we wonder how to do that. Recognizing that we cannot do it ourselves can bring us to a place of helpless and open us to receiving the Divine's help. Think of how frustrating it is for you when your children clearly need help and they shut you out. We're doing this all the time in our relationship with the Divine. See that you can't do it without help. If you could have done it yourself, you wouldn't be asking. Connect with your Divine from a place of receptivity.

Be Clear

Be specific in your request. A friend of mine who has a deep connection with his Divine followed these steps when praying for a red convertible. Sometime later, he heard a knock on the door. He opened the door to a child holding a toy car – a red convertible – saying, "This is yours." In my experience, the Divine has a sense of humor, so be clear about what you want.

Be Authentic. Speak Your Truth.

Earlier, we talked about how truth opens the heart. To create a deeper relationship with the Divine, you can simply speak your truth in the moment. The question to ask yourself then is, "Why do I want what I am praying for?"

In my corporate life, I prayed hard to get a general manager job, mostly out of jealousy for my siblings' successes and partly to get approval from my father. I would just simply include that in the prayer. It's humbling and it puts you in a state to receive.

Envision It Happening Now

The next step is to envision it happening in present time and put some feeling behind it. Remember the power of your charges when they had emotions wrapped with thoughts? All of your attention was attracted there. As more of your attention was consumed, it energized the charge. You can reverse that method here and envision yourself being this strong, spiritual support for your family and community and feel passionate about it. See it and feel it to attract energy. As more of your attention is focused there, it gains more energy, which is used to create what you are envisioning. Feel the joy of receiving what you are asking.

Often, I have prayed from a place of deficiency and fear. Usually, I waited until I desperately needed help to pray. Since I put out that energy, it attracted the same energy of desperation and lack. Like attracts like. When I was told to pray as if it were already happening, I was frustrated, because it wasn't happening. Why should I joyfully pretend that it is? I was disconnected and sitting in a level of consciousness where I was unable to receive. The fear and deficiency states are contracted. By definition, the Divine can't get through to us. Our prayer is from a place of not just believing it can happen but from a place of knowing it is already done. Envision yourself living in the reality where what you are asking for exists.

Forgive

We have worked through some obstacles earlier in the book using forgiveness. Take a few moments now and see if there is someone you need to forgive or ask forgiveness from. It doesn't have to be related to your prayer. Any place where you are experiencing a lack of forgiveness can affect your ability to receive. If there is someone you need to forgive, bring an image of the person before you, release the charge by experiencing the hurt, and then offer forgiveness. If there is someone from whom you need to ask forgiveness, bring their image before you. Feel their pain. Ask for forgiveness.

Commit

What will you offer in return for receiving this gift from the Divine? What can you commit to? This question usually stops people cold in their tracks. Our mind is designed to wriggle out of commitments. It doesn't like to be pinned down. We might be afraid of making a commitment because we have broken so many of them in the past. This is a good place to pause and review any commitments you have not lived up to and see what action you need to take. You may need to talk to the people involved, recommit, or offer a prayer. Connect inside and ask your Divine for guidance.

If you can persevere and make a commitment now, it will empower your prayer. This is a way to make your Divine your business partner in this venture. If your commitment is to help others, then you are spreading the grace to a larger group. The Divine will need to send more energy your way. It's a beautiful practice to share the wealth.

Be Grateful

The last step is to offer gratitude knowing it is done. There are many levels of gratitude, but even the simplest, heartfelt thank you is powerful. If you would like to experience a deeper level of gratitude, then imagine all that had to happen for the Divine to bring this to you. Your expression of gratitude to the Divine will come from a more powerful place.

While there are many forms of prayer, these steps that came from my Oneness teachings are the most comprehensive and powerful that I have seen:

1. Connect with your Divine.
2. Be clear and specific about what you want.
3. Be authentic and express why you want it.
4. Envision it happening now and feel it deeply.
5. Check to see if you need to forgive or ask forgiveness from anyone.
6. Commit to do something in return.
7. Offer gratitude to your Divine.

Noticing the Divine hand operating in your life more consistently will move your experience of life into something miraculous. You'll shift from a place of seeing coincidences as luck, to seeing synchronicities as the Divine plan unfolding, to opening up to miracles.

Since the mind is quick to discount the extraordinary and forget all that the Divine has done for you, it's important to write down your prayers and when they were answered. You'll see how much the Divine has done for you and you'll depend on it. Grace can do the heavy lifting.

When my friend asked me to walk the El Camino with her, I didn't know how that was going to be possible, but something deep inside said yes. I desired to do this for a few years, but I thought it would have to be in my next lifetime. While I used to be in great shape, I had not moved my body much in the past few years. At age 60, it takes longer to get back on track. None of that mattered in the moment when I felt inspired by her request. Grace had to do the heavy lifting.

A miraculous healer showed up on my doorstep to heal my knees. My daily walking routine gave me so much extra energy for everything else I did that it supported me on this book journey. My limited mind would never have said yes to training for the El Camino or to writing a book alongside my already full plate. I show up by listening to and following my guidance, and the Divine brings me all the resources I need.

Keep that prayer journal to deepen your faith and remind you that your Divine is always there for you. Write the date that you prayed, the date it was answered, and your gratitude. One of our community members has developed a great relationship with his Divine in a short period of time.

Before finding FHC, Patrick was desperate, unemployed, broke, and looking helplessly for a job. He found free meditation classes at a local yoga studio, which increased his focus and drive. Within two weeks, he received four job offers and accepted one of them. I met Patrick at this stage, in his yoga studio where I offered a special mediation class. He asked penetrating questions about connecting with Source energy and I invited him to a weekend event. After attending various processes, which deepened his bond with the Divine, he felt compelled to decline the job he had been offered and continued his search. He was beginning to trust this guidance, but it was a new experience and he needed support.

During this time of doubt and financial drought, he drove an hour each way to FHC at least once a week. I guided him though two more excruciating months of job hunting. Using the seven-step prayer, meditation and the ancestor process, he started to become more alive and aware of all the synchronicities happening for him. He prayed for a job that used his talents and fulfilled him. During that time, he received five more offers. Each week, he would talk about turning down another job because it didn't feel right. On the eighth week, he showed up beaming. The perfect job landed in his lap. He completely trusted his Divine in this process, which took tremendous courage and persistence.

Now that you have the keys to a strong relationship with your Divine and the methods for asking what for what you want, you can use it to create magic in the lives of people around you.

Chapter 11

REALIZE YOU ARE
THAT STRONG SUPPORT

"The outer world is a reflection of the inner world."
~ Sri Bhagavan ~

As you continue to go deeper in your practices, your heart opens, and you will naturally be that strong support for your family. In this chapter, we'll look at extending your support to family members who have passed. Even if you don't know them, you can develop a relationship that will bring you joy and have a powerful impact on your life. Your family and work relationships will become more fulfilling. You may want to start giving back by sharing your experiences with others and gathering a small group or a community. It's important to have people around you who are also working on their spiritual growth.

Being that strong support for family and community starts with being that for yourself and learning to let the Divine lead the way. You may already notice some changes in how you are interacting with your family. As you continue to open your heart, face the truth and follow your guidance, your whole experience of life shifts. You see it reflected in your relationships. It takes commitment to keep going. It might seem like there are more upheavals or disturbances happening, because feelings and experiences that you have suppressed will begin surfacing. As you follow your guidance and your truth, some things that you think are necessary may fall away, but they are not actually serving you right now. Trust the process. Learn to expect the unexpected.

One of our strong supporters over the years, Yolanda, made an intention to heal all of her relationships. She experienced a lifelong feeling of not belonging in her family of origin, which appeared to be the result of rejection from her sister and nieces. Yolanda's persistence and courage to see the truth led her to discover that, through her judgments and fears, she literally separated herself from her family. As she worked through her charges and connected more deeply with her Divine, the barriers between her and her family lifted quite miraculously. Now her family wants to be around her because they feel welcomed and accepted for who they are.

I used to pursue spirituality because I wanted relief from suffering. My mind is strong and fearful thoughts tortured me. It seemed that those in high states of consciousness were in bliss. and that's where I wanted to be. Our yearly trips to Hawaii were my attempt to produce those feelings, but the joy was fleeting.

On this path, I had many blissful experiences and I also faced some difficulties. I learned how to depend on the Divine for support rather than my bank account. I sat in the face of criticism from my loved ones and looked at the truth of what they were saying – that I was selfish, cold, and distant. I have been targeted and betrayed and did that to others. I finally discovered that it was more painful to cover up these behaviors than to see them. The freedom that I experience now was worth it. I was willing to see where I was mean or self-serving, and, in the process, became more compassionate and giving. The relief that comes from spirituality is in the form of a grounded, peaceful acceptance rather than blissful escape. I am free to be me. I couldn't do this alone. I don't recommend being alone on this path.

Community

I needed a community of people to reflect back to me what I couldn't see. When I joined the Shematrix Mystery School, I thought I was going to learn magic and secret information. Instead, I unlearned and unraveled. A strong group of women held me to my commitments. It was all done in such a field of love that even when they wielded their swords, the destruction was healing. Throughout my life, I built up many walls of protection and hid my voice deep inside. Through the process of seeing and speaking my truth, I found my voice again.

Through the Oneness Community, I rekindled my faith and developed such a strong relationship with my Divine that miracles happened for me. In that high consciousness field in India, my brain shifted and awakened. I could experience such a deep connection with others easily. I remember sitting with my husband one day when he was upset. I started to respond from a triggered place. All of a sudden, I found myself inside his shoes, experiencing his pain. I was in such a state of shock and sadness that, instead of delivering that retort, I said I was sorry. This has happened many times now, where I experience the pain the other is sitting with and I can respond with compassion despite whatever words they are shouting at me. It starts with becoming completely one within ourselves and accepting all aspects, even the shadow aspects we explored in the forgiveness chapter. When we are whole, we can experience what the other is sitting in easier and respond with loving actions.

Being That Strong Support

Being there for others requires you to be there for yourself first and foremost. Committing to a practice to keep your space clear is critical. We've covered several here:

- Start with setting a strong intention.

- Connect with your Divine and talk with them as often as you can.

- Become aware of whether you are in a connected, inspired state, or disconnected and spiraling down. Shift if necessary.

- Anytime you are triggered, feel what is being activated in you.

- If you forget to do that in the moment, look back at your hurts at the end of the day and experience the charges. See the meditation below.

- If there are aspects of you that you still can't accept, go through the forgiveness process.

- Recognize your awareness deepening through the witness meditation daily.

- Find other periods of time, preferably one to two days per month where you can be in silence to increase awareness and allow your brain to integrate your experiences

- Keep a prayer journal and celebrate when they are answered.

- Do the evening meditation below.

- Expect miracles.

- I highly recommend this meditation as a daily practice.

Evening Meditation from Oneness

"Decharge and capture the beauty."

1. Capture and review the magic moments of the day.

   - Invoke the presence and stack your memories with all the good and great experiences of the day. See them, feel them, associate to them, and feel gratitude.

2. Ask yourself if you gave pain to anyone today.

   - If so, invoke the presence, feel their pain, and ask for forgiveness by bringing the image of that person before you.

3. Ask yourself if you feel any pain from your interactions with others.

   - Invoke the presence.

   - Affirm the truth – "all pain is not in the facts, but in my perception of the facts." The pain is not outside, it's inside. Changing it, blaming it, or distracting yourself from it will not eliminate the source of your pain.

   - Feel the pain. Stay with it until it becomes forgiveness or joy.

4. Bless all those who have touched your life today.

   - Invoke the presence. Bring before you images and faces of everyone who has touched you today. Bless them and give them thanks.

Sacredness

As an outward reminder of your inner relationship with the Divine, create an altar in your home and, if possible, your work space. Place a photo of your Divine or something that represents it, like a candle, incense, and flowers when you can. That space will start to create a beautiful energy in your home. For that to happen, it needs attention. Light the candle each day, say a prayer there, and leave offerings. Your home will feel more sacred. This is the best place to keep your prayer journal.

In our center, we have a sacred chamber – a permanent space dedicated to the Divine – maintained with candles, sacred chants, and flowers. It contains a picture of the Supreme Light, representing the Divine in whatever form you desire. I was initiated in India to offer a specific process to bring people to a place of humility, reverence, and gratitude in preparation for experiencing the sacred space in the chamber Many miracles occurred in the few minutes they were in the chamber. A few people with troubled family relationships were shown the life story of the person with whom they were struggling. This led to such a deep compassion for the person and their circumstance that the relationship completely shifted. Others had questions answered or physical healings. This is the power of a sacred space.

Sacredness is not something I was taught growing up. I found it in the church where we had to dress appropriately and behave in a reverent way. I didn't understand it then, but I felt the power of the energy there. Entering into a relationship with the Divine is sacred, so treating the altar with sacredness will support you in coming from that place. In a sense, everything around us is sacred, but it requires us to meet it from a place of sacredness inside ourselves. Candles, incense, and flowers help bring out the sacredness in us and make the connection to the Divine so much stronger. As this quality develops, you will begin to treat all life with sacredness. You will naturally take better care of your environment. From that place of sacredness, you'll glimpse the mystery of life that is unfolding around you. The more you stay in that place of unknown, the more alive everything appears.

The simple act of creating an altar, lighting candles and offering flowers, food, and incense is the beginning of a ritual. Since ancient times, peoples have done this to recognize, invoke, and honor the Divine. As this practice goes back thousands of years, it has worn a deep groove in our consciousnesses. Something inside of us becomes activated and alert to the presence in a powerful way. I love doing rituals to increase my connection to the Divine and to connect with my ancestors.

Ancestors

I often call in my ancestors at the beginning of a class that I offer or a project that I do to honor them and thank them. When I learned the importance of having a great relationship with my ancestors and helping to liberate them, I was intrigued. This was a new concept for me. While I believed in reincarnation, I thought that when they passed, our "relationship" was over. I still had the good memories and the photos. I learned in India that any issues in my ancestral line (e.g. my dad with his dad) could create trouble in my life. I didn't fully appreciate how I am an extension of my ancestors and that their unresolved issues are in my field. Fortunately, they respond easily and quickly to prayers of gratitude and forgiveness. I loved praying for them to move to higher realms.

One time, I decided to connect with my mother's aunt during the process. I had never met her, but I knew my mom had a special connection with her. At the time, I was having trouble with my mom. I prayed to my great aunt, Laura, during the process and asked for help with my relationship with my mom. I figured she would be the expert there. After that process, I visited my mom and she said, "There is a box in the basement with glasses that belonged to my Aunt Laura. You should have them." This shocked me. My mother had been in that house for more than 35 years and that box, along with others, remained unopened and untouched.

Recently, after my mom's passing, I decided to do a Mother's Day ritual. I gathered all my ancestors' photos that I could find and put them on an altar. I remembered that I was wearing the ring of my great grandmother, Annie, whom I had never met. I had only seen her photo once, when my nephew helped me clean the basement. I asked him to put it aside for me to look at more closely later. For three weeks, I looked for that photo and couldn't find it. I told Annie that if she wanted to be part of this ritual, that I needed to find that photo. That morning, I drove to my mom's and walked right to the correct box in the basement. Her photo was on top when I lifted the lid. I thanked her and then asked for more information about who she was. I continued digging into the boxes and found an article written in 1932 by her friend, describing Annie's character. I thought I might find an obituary, but never expected to find that kind of article. I enjoyed this new relationship with my ancestors and still do. I ask them for help with my family relationships and I feel supported and connected.

You might want to place photos of your ancestors on your altar and bring them consciously into your life. I learned in India that it's my job to liberate them. You can pray to your Divine for their liberation. As you step into this role of being that spiritual support for your family, recognize that it includes those that have already passed, and you'll be surprised by the impact in your life.

Creating Your Community

As you grow, you'll naturally want to give back to your community. We need each other to see what we cannot see on our own so we can keep growing. We are all in this together. Everyone has his or her unique expertise and voice. Start listening to what is needed in your community and what your friends or community members need and support them. This practice will help you grow.

There is an art to listening. It includes being fully present with others in the community and simultaneously listening to what is happening within you. Much of the time, we are either completely over in in the other person's space, vacating our body and wisdom, or we withdraw from them because we are wrapped up in our thoughts. Listening means to stay fully connected inside while listening to them. Ask for guidance and your response will be what is needed in the situation.

I started a weekly group about seven years ago to provide extra support for those who were on their spiritual journey. I thought I did this as a service. Over the years, I received as much support from them as they have from me. All the regulars have been with me that entire time. We help each other through life challenges and to grow in creative and inspiring ways.

We use a simple format. We might start with a teaching and discuss it. Then, each person gets a few minutes to speak about two topics. One is what they are grateful for or where they have seen growth in themselves, and the other is what they would like support with. Everyone uses that technique for listening, and if they have a response, they ask permission to offer it. Then, the group either sends a blessing (sending golden Divine energy) or prays for them. We close by sending prayers or blessings to others in need. If you feel called to extend your spiritual leadership to a community, this is one great way to start.

Now that you have a sense of the scope of this leadership role, what's next?

Chapter 12

JOURNEY ALONE OR WITH COMPANIONS

You now have a sense of the overall journey to become that strong, spiritual support for your family, and the steps along the way. You can certainly take this journey on your own. Many have done that. You also know what it's like to be there for others. You have been there to pick up your children when they fall and hurt themselves. It feels good to offer that support, especially when they are open to receiving it.

You may need that same support. Who picks you up when you fall? This journey is a trip into the unknown. Twists and turns and pitfalls are all part of it. For critical life junctures, I always had a guide – someone who showed up to be there for me, listening and offering a helping hand. I didn't even fully realize this until I started writing this book. The Divine has sent me support every time in the form a beautiful human being.

Fear

This path is unpredictable. It naturally surfaces your fears and sabotaging patterns. At that point, you can buy into those fears and be swept along by your patterns, spiraling down into more density. Or, you can choose to face it, see and experience what is there, and expand out of it. There is no middle ground.

Your fears have no substance. If you lean into them rather than running from them, you'll see them recede and disappear. It's expected to have fear as your companion when entering unknown territory. Practice consciously allowing the energy of fear to run through your system and notice how it feels. I experience it like cold electricity. When I allow this energy to flow, it doesn't last long. I had months where I awoke every morning to this freight train of fear running through my system. It was during one of the times I had stretched myself beyond what I thought I could do. I wasn't fully trusting my Divine yet. Each morning, I awoke to it and lay there, allowing the energy to flow full force through my body for a few minutes. When it was complete, I would get up and go about my day without any trace of fear. On days where I forgot and bought into the fear, it was with me all day long.

There are a few other obstacles to be aware of in this particular path. The first is thinking, "I know." The mind can't stand being in the unknown, so it's quick to measure, categorize, and conclude. "I know what this is. I've done this before." If you buy into this, you cut the connection with your Divine and any guidance you receive will mislead you. How many times have you ignored your intuition and paid the price? If the mind says, "I know," stop, breathe, and reconnect with the Divine.

One woman who used to come to our center would say, "I know" to everything anyone said. When she did that with me, at first, I felt unheard. I then realized her mind was too busy and she was too full of thoughts. She was more focused on what she wanted to get across, than listening. Talking with her was like pouring more water into an already full cup. It's impossible. She consistently worked on experiencing what she felt without judgment, and this created space for more input. One day, she stopped saying, "I know."

Another consequence of this "I know" stance is that it creates conflict. Once you become positional in relating to your family members, you disconnect from them and the Divine. You aren't listening to their side of the story and they feel it. A conflict is inevitable. You can observe this with your family. Take a position on something and, even if they agree with your point, they will take the opposite view. It's automatic. Becoming positional leads to righteousness, blaming, and conflict.

Another common obstacle is hidden agendas. The mind is clever and knows how to use your spiritual knowledge to trip you up in more subtle ways. You might think you are deeply listening to someone without judgment, but if you are holding an agenda for a certain outcome, you are again disconnected from your Divine and the result will create more conflict for both of you. I experienced this when I have tried to talk my husband into doing something he didn't want to do. I listened to what he was experiencing and suggested he see a chiropractor. I guilted him into it because I was frustrated watching him in pain and wanted him and me to get some relief. Of course, in this case, the appointment didn't help him.

As your awareness grows, you'll start to see what is really happening. Your desire to show up as that spiritual support and your willingness to see where you have work to do are important. The mind is very used to hiding its agendas and manipulation. One way to increase your awareness of its tricks is to sit in mediation and watch.

I noticed in this exercise that even the simplest statements can have a hidden agenda. Sometimes, when I say, "I love you," it's because I feel alone and want to hear the other person say, "I love you." It would be better in that case to tell the other person how I am feeling instead of setting this expectation.

Integrity Process

Set an intention to see the ways the mind manipulates, lies, covers up, and isolates you from seeing the truth.

Ask for support from your Divine.

Sit for 49 minutes and go back through the day.

Find all the lies the mind has told you. You will be amazed.

If you do this process for 21 days, your awareness of the mind's activities will increase significantly, and you can start to avoid some of these obstacles.

As you go deeper into your journey, the tricks of the mind become more and more subtle. The danger of thinking that you are further along in your process than you actually are is very high. This is where community is essential. In a family situation, you are constantly getting feedback and you can use that. In a spiritual community, you can invite feedback from those who speak the same language and have had similar experiences. Their insights are invaluable in supporting you. Everything is magnified in a group, so the learning and growth come much faster.

I was in a situation where I thought I was following my guidance, but I was actually buying into fear. I was invited into a pyramid scheme disguised as something more spiritual, and I jumped at it. I needed money to keep the center going and I thought this would be a way out. The thing that should have tipped me off was my reluctance to tell my Mystery School sisters. I had many reasons for why that wasn't necessary. Because I kept it hidden, I wasn't as effective in my work and they wondered why. When they found out, they were furious with me for breaking their trust, abusing my power, and keeping it secret. I had to squarely face the consequences of my betrayal, hearing from each of my sisters how it affected her. Again, there was a field of love present as each person reached deeply inside and spoke her truth. That was one of my hardest lessons. I would never have seen what I was doing without their help because my mind was operating out of fear and covering it up with spiritual concepts. I experienced inner healing and my guidance became clearer and stronger.

Many people keep rushing through their lives thinking that some form of "success" will bring them the happiness that they constantly seeking. They don't know there is another way. Now, you know that what you are seeking is not out there. The happiness is always, always sourced within. The ability to support others and accept them as they are comes from an ability to do that for yourself

Through this journey, you will have a stronger, clearer connection to your inner guidance system and learn to trust it. When you move through your fears and other obstacles to take action in your life from a heart-centered place, your relationships will heal and your life will be become more fulfilling. When you burst through your mental strategies and start living a miraculous life, you'll never want to go back. You'll find it hard to watch others in pain, knowing there is a better way. You will naturally reach out to help others around you live a more fulfilling life.

Chapter 13

CONCLUSION

This is the book I wish I had in my hands when I was younger and running into some big life questions. I was so focused on my success and taking care of my family to the best of my ability that I didn't even think to look inside. It didn't occur to me how impactful forgiveness and acceptance practices would be for my family. I thought it was selfish to spend time working on myself because I didn't understand the larger impact. I thought the inner world was separate and hidden from the outer world.

Now, many years later, I see the bigger picture. I see that we are all giving our children messages of a spiritual nature whether we realize it. Even if we send them to parochial schools or catechism class, they learn about relationships and forgiveness from us. With the young adults I see coming into our center, I notice how much pressure they feel to live up to society and family expectations. They are bombarded with media and information from every direction telling them what to do and how to act. They seek grounding in the basic skills of life – how to deal with hurts, how to love and accept themselves, how to forgive others. The quality of their life depends on the quality of their relationships.

You must start with your own inner journey and create inner stability, so your family has a solid foundation to lean on. Whether you are raising a family, managing teams at work, or leading a community, it's critical to come to a place of deep inner peace, love, and connection to your higher intelligence. The world will be a happier place when we all cooperate more than we compete, when we look at how alike we are instead of focusing on the differences.

Let this book be your guide. Continue to use these tools so you can move through your fears and other obstacles to take action in your life from a more heart-centered place. You'll know in your heart that you are doing everything you can to support your family's happiness and well-being. You will be able to help them handle their life challenges in clear and effective ways without being knocked off-center. Whether the children go to a private school or a parochial school, they will be getting what they most need at home: deep love, acceptance of who they are, and self-esteem that comes from knowing their place in the world.

Remember to follow the Flowering Heart Processes. Take time out for yourself frequently with three deep, slow breaths, and look at what is happening in your life right now. Don't live in the fantasy world of the future. Rather, see your current state of well-being.

Decide what experience you prefer to have for yourself and your family and set a powerful intention. Have frequent conversations with your Divine. Stay connected and follow the guidance you receive. Do the evening meditation to clear hurts from your day, forgive others and bless everyone who has crossed your path.

Stay aware of whether you are in a state of connection. If you are disconnected, don't interact with others until you shift back into connection. Notice when you are triggered and be present to feelings moving through. Listen deeply with your full presence when others are speaking, so you can respond from a place that is healing for both of you. Schedule periods of silence to let your brain process information and get closer to your Divine. Practice moving into the witness state so you can see the bigger picture and experience more of that deep inner peace. Then, expect miracles! Let grace do the heavy lifting, share what you notice, and offer gratitude to spirit.

And finally, give back. Gather a small group of people and meet regularly. Each of you can share what is happening in your lives and use the powerful prayer that you have learned in this book. Being with others helps you see yourself from a different viewpoint. You'll receive as much support as you are giving by being that guide for others.

And, remember that you are already that strong, spiritual leader for your family and community. Keep going and experience the joy that comes from a consistent, powerful connection with Source.

Feel good about yourself, knowing in your heart that you do everything you can to support your family's happiness and well-being.

You will be able to handle their life challenges in a clear and effective way without being knocked off-center.

Learning and growth is a continuous journey with no destination. As long as you keep growing, so will your family and community.

ACKNOWLEDGMENTS

Thank you to the Shematrix Mystery School and my sisters who patiently stood by me while I unlearned the troublesome behaviors that seemingly worked for me in the corporate world. Thank you to my trainers, Kisha and Marsha, for taking on the daunting task of transforming me into someone who loves being of service in the world and who can powerfully hold sacred space. I could never have created a spiritual community without all I have learned from this collective of women.

Thank you to Sri Amma and Sri Bhagavan and all the powerful teachings and processes for awakening that I experienced at Oneness University and continue to experience through The Golden Age Movement. You have a special place in my heart, and I am in deep gratitude for helping me find my faith, a deep level of trust, and openness to a miraculous life.

Thank you to my Flowering Heart Center Board members and the community for all of your love, support, and dedication to raising consciousness. A special thank you to our Thursday morning

Satsang group for sticking with me all these years and for encouraging each other to continue to grow.

Huge gratitude and love to my husband Frank for your continual encouragement and your belief in my abilities. I feel loved and supported.

A huge thank you to my children, Kara and Kevin, who have put up with the huge shift in our lives and lifestyles that occurred when I switched from my corporate job to the personal growth world. Thank you for being an inspiration for me to continue to grow and create community.

To Byron Katie, whose work and schooling heavily influenced my personal growth journey.

To Sonia Choquette, one of my first teachers to work with me on developing my intuition, for reminding me to focus on how alike we are instead of looking for differences, and for the instruction to keep dancing.

To Laura Jane at Yoga Among Friends for planting the seed in my consciousness for creating a center in my home. To Janice Cadwell, an extraordinary yoga teacher, for helping me to stretch beyond what I thought possible.

To Dr. Basha Kaplan, my guide through a tumultuous time in my life and for teaching me about conscious relationships.

To Rev. Dr. Michael Milner for ordaining me, inspiring me and for his continued guidance and wisdom.

To all the spiritual teachers who have regularly shared their teachings and powerful presence at FHC, including Mirabai Devi, Atma Nambi, John Newton, Doug Bentley.

To Catherine Scherwenka, for allowing me to partner with her in the Freedom Through Forgiveness course, some elements of which are in here. Thank you for being the catalyst for this book by introducing me to Dr. Angela.

To Dr. Angela and her team at The Author Incubator, for creating such a powerful program that works for me. I have been talking about writing books for a long time but thought I needed to wait until I had a lot of space in my calendar. I love your transformational approach.

To all my spirit guides for taking me on a magical journey through life.

THANK YOU

Thank you for reading my book! As a way of saying thank you for reaching out, I'd like to offer you a free 30-minute class on being that strong spiritual support for your family and community. Since this path is about learning to navigate in the face of unknowns, I'm happy to be your guide for a while longer.

Visit **www.FloweringHeartCenter.org/Thank-you** today, grab a cup of tea, and continue your journey with me.

ABOUT THE AUTHOR

KRISTIN PANEK is the founder and spiritual director of the Flowering Heart Center, a not-for-profit organization that creates sacred space for community healing and transformation into higher states of consciousness. She offers counseling and workshops for this community of over 500 members. She is an ordained interfaith minister of the Seraphic Order of the Flowering Heart.

She is a heart-centered, spiritual empowerment mentor, teacher, and international speaker. By transforming deeply-rooted beliefs and fostering the connection to the Divine within, she supports soul-seekers on their awakening path to step into their fullest potential.

She is also a licensed guide with Shematrix, a collective of women who sponsor transformational events for women and men that involve a rite of initiation into the Divine Feminine. She has been a part of their mystery school for eighteen years.

She is also an advanced trainer, national coordinator, and a sacred chamber facilitator in The Oneness Movement. She has been involved with Oneness since 2008. She has taken groups to India and has been there twelve times receiving teachings and various initiations.

She is a licensed avatar master and delivers training on a series of tools for managing consciousness and creating preferred realities. She is also a sixth sensory practitioner, licensed by Sonia Choquette, and a facilitator for The Work of Byron Katie. Kristin is also a meditation guide, a certified yoga instructor, master herbalist and reiki master.

DIFFERENCE
PRESS

ABOUT DIFFERENCE PRESS

Difference Press is the exclusive publishing arm of The Author Incubator, an educational company for entrepreneurs – including life coaches, healers, consultants, and community leaders – looking for a comprehensive solution to get their books written, published, and promoted. Its founder, Dr. Angela Lauria, has been bringing to life the literary ventures of hundreds of authors-in-transformation since 1994.

A boutique-style self-publishing service for clients of The Author Incubator, Difference Press boasts a fair and easy-to-understand profit structure, low-priced author copies, and author-friendly contract terms. Most importantly, all of our #incubatedauthors maintain ownership of their copyright at all times.

Let's Start a Movement with Your Message

In a market where hundreds of thousands of books are published every year and are never heard from again, The Author Incubator is different. Not only do all Difference Press books reach Amazon bestseller status, but all of our authors are actively changing lives and making a difference.

Since launching in 2013, we've served over 500 authors who came to us with an idea for a book and were able to write it and get it self-published in less than 6 months. In addition, more than 100 of those books were picked up by traditional publishers and are now available in book stores. We do this by selecting the highest quality and highest potential applicants for our future programs.

Our program doesn't only teach you how to write a book – our team of coaches, developmental editors, copy editors, art directors, and marketing experts incubate you from having a book idea to being a published, bestselling author, ensuring that the book you create can actually make a difference in the world. Then we give you the training you need to use your book to make the difference in the world, or to create a business out of serving your readers.

Are You Ready to Make a Difference?

You've seen other people make a difference with a book. Now it's your turn. If you are ready to stop watching and start taking massive action, go to http://theauthorincubator.com/apply/.

"Yes, I'm ready!"

OTHER BOOKS
BY DIFFERENCE PRESS

---

*The Right Franchise for You: Escape the 9 to 5,
Generate Wealth, & Live Life on Your Terms*
by Faizun Kamal

*Overcome Thyroid Symptoms & Love Your Life:
The Personal Guide to Renewal & Re-Calibration*
by Vannette Keast

*The Luminary Journey: Lessons from a Volcano in
Creating a Healing Center and Becoming the
Leader You Were Born to Be*
by Darshan Mendoza

*The End Is Near: Planning the Life You Want
after the Kids Are Gone*
by Amie Eyre Newhouse

When Marriage Needs an Answer: The Decision to Fix Your Struggling Marriage or Leave Without Regret by Sharon Pope

*Leadership through Trust & Collaboration:
Practical Tools for Today's Results-Driven Leader*
by Jill Ratliff

*Conquer Foot Pain: The Art of Eliminating Pain by Improving
Posture so You Can Exercise Again*
by Julie Renae Smith, MPT

*The Art of Connected Leadership: The Manager's Guide
for Keeping Rock Stars and Building Powerhouse Teams*
by Lyndsay K.R. Toensing

Financial Freedom for Six-Figure Entrepreneurs:
Lower Taxes, Build Wealth, Create Your Best Life
by Jennifer Vavricka

BAD (Begin Again Differently):
7 Smart Processes to Win Again after Suffering a Business Loss
by Claudette Yarbrough